Family Casseroles

Family
Casseroles

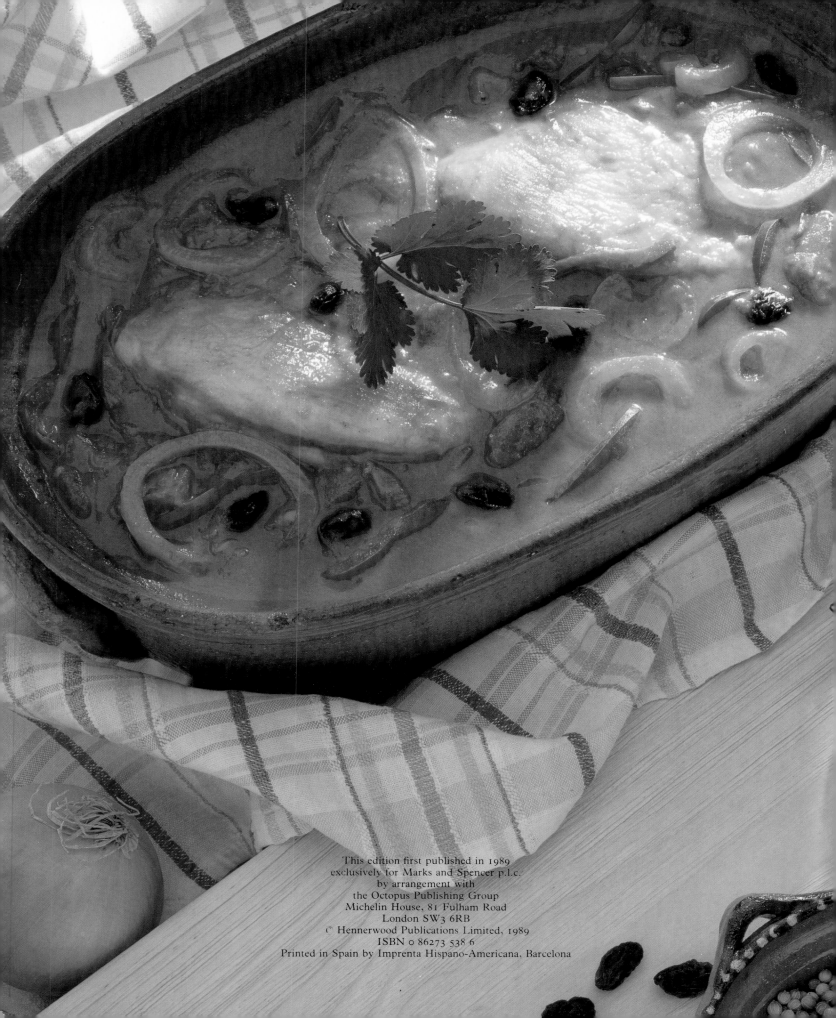

This edition first published in 1989
exclusively for Marks and Spencer p.l.c.
by arrangement with
the Octopus Publishing Group
Michelin House, 81 Fulham Road
London SW3 6RB
© Hennerwood Publications Limited, 1989
ISBN 0 86273 538 6
Printed in Spain by Imprenta Hispano-Americana, Barcelona

Contents

Beef & veal

◆

CASSEROLES

For family meals or easy and casual entertaining, nothing can beat a casserole. This method of cooking is ideal for the more economical cuts of beef and veal – braising and stewing steak, minced beef, pie veal, oxtail – and it's an excellent way to use up leftover roasted meat, too.

The recipes in this chapter range from simple combinations of beef or veal, vegetables and stock to more unusual casseroles flavoured with subtly spicy green peppercorns, apples and curry powder, horseradish cream, or hot mustard and Worcestershire sauce. There's a rich casserole of beef and pheasant with wine and cranberries, and a more delicate dish of veal with artichoke hearts and rosemary. And there are all-in-one casseroles that include pasta, rice or potatoes, which need only a simple salad to accompany them.

TOP: Beef & Pheasant Casserole (see recipe on page 8);
BOTTOM: Braised Veal with Artichoke Hearts (see recipe on page 11).

BEEF & PHEASANT CASSEROLE

2 tablespoons vegetable oil or dripping
1 oven-ready pheasant, jointed into 8 pieces
450g (1lb) best-quality braising steak, trimmed of
  excess fat and cut into 2.5cm (1 inch) cubes
2 large onions, peeled and cut into eighths
2 tablespoons plain flour
150ml ($\frac{1}{4}$ pint) dry white wine
450ml ($\frac{3}{4}$ pint) beef stock
1 tablespoon red wine vinegar
salt
freshly ground black pepper
$\frac{1}{2}$ teaspoon dried thyme
4 tablespoons whole-berry cranberry sauce
100g (4oz) button mushrooms, sliced

Preparation time: 30 minutes
Cooking time: 2$\frac{1}{4}$ hours
Oven: 160°C, 325°F, Gas Mark 3

1. Heat the oil in a frying pan, add the pheasant pieces and fry over a moderate heat, turning often, until well browned. Transfer to a casserole.
2. Reheat the oil in the pan, add the beef cubes and fry, turning often, until well sealed and browned on all sides. Add to the casserole.
3. Add the onions to the pan and fry over a gentle heat for 5 minutes until lightly coloured. Sprinkle in the flour, stir well and fry for a further 1–2 minutes. Gradually stir in the wine, stock and vinegar and bring to the boil. Season well with salt and pepper, add the thyme and cranberry sauce and heat gently, stirring, until the sauce has melted.
4. Pour the contents of the pan into the casserole, cover and cook in a preheated oven for about 2 hours or until the pheasant and beef are tender. Add the mushrooms 30 minutes before the end of the cooking time. Taste and adjust the seasoning. Serve with creamed potatoes and Brussels sprouts.

Serves 4

Nutrition content per serving   Carbohydrate: 21g   Fat: 19g
Fibre: 2g   Kilocalories: 422

DEVILLED VEAL

50g (2oz) butter
750g (1$\frac{1}{2}$ lb) stewing veal, cubed
2 leeks, white part only, sliced
25g (1oz) plain flour
350ml (12fl oz) stock
225g (8oz) parsnips, peeled and cubed
225g (8oz) carrots, peeled and sliced
2 tablespoons tomato ketchup
2 teaspoons made mustard
2 teaspoons Worcestershire sauce
salt
freshly ground black pepper
225g (8oz) tomatoes, skinned and sliced
4 streaky bacon rashers, rind removed, halved
fried sliced mushrooms, to garnish

Preparation time: 25 minutes
Cooking time: 1$\frac{1}{2}$ hours
Oven: 180°C, 350°F, Gas Mark 4

1. Melt the butter in a flameproof casserole, add the veal and brown on all sides.
2. Stir in the leeks and cook gently for 5 minutes.
3. Mix in the flour and cook for 2 minutes. Stir in the stock and bring slowly to the boil.
4. Add the parsnips, carrots, tomato ketchup, mustard and Worcestershire sauce. Season to taste with salt and pepper.
5. Cover and transfer to a preheated oven. Cook for 1 hour.
6. Stir in the tomatoes. Roll up the bacon rashers and place on top of the casserole.
7. Return to the oven, uncovered, and continue cooking for 30 minutes or until the bacon rolls are crisp on top. Garnish with mushrooms.

Serves 4

Nutrition content per serving   Carbohydrate: 19g   Fat: 29g
Fibre: 6g   Kilocalories: 516

Devilled Veal.

BEEF WITH GREEN PEPPERCORNS

2 tablespoons vegetable oil
1kg (2lb) chuck steak, trimmed of excess fat and
*   cut into large chunks*
1 large onion, peeled and chopped
2–3 celery sticks, chopped
1 garlic clove, peeled and crushed
4 streaky bacon rashers, rinds removed, chopped
3 tablespoons green peppercorns, drained
3 tablespoons chopped fresh parsley
300ml (½ pint) dry white wine
150ml (¼ pint) beef stock or water
2 bay leaves
salt

Preparation time: 30 minutes
Cooking time: 2–2½ hours
Oven: 160°C, 325°F, Gas Mark 3

1. Heat the oil in a large flameproof casserole, add the meat and fry over brisk heat until browned on all sides. Remove with a slotted spoon and drain on paper towels.
2. Lower the heat and add the onion, celery, garlic and bacon to the casserole. Fry gently until the vegetables are softened and the bacon lightly coloured, stirring constantly with a wooden spoon.
3. Crush 2 tablespoons peppercorns in a mortar and pestle, then stir into the casserole with 2 tablespoons parsley. Fry for 2–3 minutes, stirring, then return the beef to the casserole.
4. Stir in the wine and stock or water and bring to the boil. Add the bay leaves and salt to taste, then cover with a tight-fitting lid. Transfer to a preheated oven and cook for 1½–2 hours or until the beef is tender.
5. Remove from the oven and discard the bay leaves. Taste and adjust the seasoning, then sprinkle with the remaining peppercorns and parsley.

Serves 4

Nutrition content per serving   Carbohydrate: 2g   Fat: 30g
Fibre: 1g   Kilocalories: 478

BRAISED VEAL WITH ARTICHOKE HEARTS

4 fillets of veal, about 100g (4oz) each
75g (3oz) butter
1 small onion, peeled and thinly sliced
1 garlic clove, peeled and crushed
50g (2oz) button mushrooms, sliced
1 teaspoon dried rosemary, crumbled
200ml (⅓ pint) white wine or dry cider
1 × 400g (14oz) can artichoke hearts, drained
*   and halved*
salt
freshly ground black pepper
1 teaspoon plain flour
4 tablespoons double cream
halved lime slices, to garnish (optional)

Preparation time: 10 minutes
Cooking time: 50 minutes
Oven: 160°C, 325°F, Gas Mark 3

1. Cut each veal fillet into 3 pieces. Fry in 25g (1oz) of the butter over moderate heat for 2 minutes on each side. Transfer the veal to a flameproof casserole.
2. Fry the onion in 25g (1oz) butter for 2 minutes. Add the garlic and mushrooms, stir well and fry for a further 2 minutes. Transfer to the casserole.
3. Add the rosemary, wine or cider and artichoke hearts to the pan, bring to the boil, and add salt and pepper. Pour into the casserole and cook in a preheated oven for 30 minutes.
4. Beat together the flour and the remaining butter to make a paste. Remove the casserole from the oven, stir the paste into the liquor and bring to the boil on top of the cooker. Simmer for 2–3 minutes, until the sauce has thickened.
5. Stir in the cream and allow to heat, without boiling. Taste and adjust the seasoning, if necessary. Garnish with lime slices, if liked.
6. New potatoes and spinach make good accompaniments.

Serves 4

Nutrition content per serving   Carbohydrate: 6g   Fat: 25g
Fibre: 1g   Kilocalories: 350

Beef with Green Peppercorns.

SHEPHERD'S PIE

50g (2oz) butter
1 large onion, peeled and chopped
2 carrots, peeled and chopped
1 tablespoon plain flour
300ml ($\frac{1}{2}$ pint) beef stock
1 tablespoon tomato purée
Worcestershire sauce
$\frac{1}{2}$ teaspoon dried mixed herbs
salt
freshly ground black pepper
450g (1lb) lean cooked beef or lamb, coarsely
    minced
450g (1lb) potatoes, peeled
top of the milk or single cream
beaten egg, to glaze

Preparation time: 30 minutes
Cooking time: 1$\frac{1}{4}$–1$\frac{1}{2}$ hours
Oven: 220°C, 425°F, Gas Mark 7

1. Melt half of the butter in a saucepan and fry the onion and carrots until golden brown. Stir in the flour and cook for 1 minute. Gradually stir in the stock and bring to the boil, stirring.
2. Add the tomato purée, Worcestershire sauce to taste, herbs and seasoning. Cover the pan, reduce the heat and simmer for 15 minutes.
3. Remove from the heat and add the cold meat. Mix well, and taste and adjust the

seasoning. Turn into an ovenproof dish.
4. Cook the potatoes in boiling water and drain. Mash or sieve the potatoes and beat in the remaining butter, and milk and seasoning to taste. Pipe the potato over the meat or spread it over with a fork, fluffing it up to give an attractive finish.
5. Brush the potato topping with beaten egg and bake in a preheated oven for 20–30 minutes, or until the topping is brown and the meat heated through.

Serves 4

Nutrition content per serving   Carbohydrate: 28g   Fat: 18g
Fibre: 3g   Kilocalories: 413

AMERICAN BEEF & CHEESE BAKE

2 tablespoons oil
450g (1lb) minced beef
1 medium onion, peeled and finely chopped
1 celery stick, finely chopped
1 × 275g (10oz) can condensed tomato soup
salt
freshly ground black pepper
75g (3oz) cottage cheese
75g (3oz) full fat soft cheese
2 tablespoons soured cream
100g (4oz) ribbon noodles, cooked and drained
fresh coriander sprig, to garnish

Preparation time: 20 minutes
Cooking time: 1 hour
Oven: 150°C, 300°F, Gas Mark 2

1. Heat the oil in a large frying pan, add the beef, onion and celery and cook over a brisk heat to brown the meat.
2. Drain off the surplus fat, then stir in the undiluted soup. Season lightly with salt and pepper and bring very gently to the boil.
3. Remove from the heat and mix in the cottage and soft cheeses, soured cream and the noodles. Check the seasoning.
4. Pour the mixture into a casserole. Cover and bake in a preheated oven for 1 hour. Serve hot, garnished with a coriander sprig.

Serves 4

Nutrition content per serving   Carbohydrate: 31g   Fat: 45g
Fibre: 2g   Kilocalories: 637

LEFT: Shepherd's Pie.
RIGHT: American Beef & Cheese Bake.

SPANISH RICE

This makes a filling, tasty supper. If you have no leftover roast beef, use any cooked meat or smoked sausage.

100g (4oz) long-grain rice
salt
2 tablespoons oil
1 large Spanish onion, peeled and sliced
225g (8oz) tomatoes, skinned and quartered
225g (8oz) roast beef, chopped
50g (2oz) mushrooms, chopped
2 tablespoons tomato purée
½ teaspoon dried oregano
freshly ground black pepper
50g (2oz) Cheddar cheese, grated
flat-leaf parsley sprig, to garnish

Preparation time: 25 minutes
Cooking time: 40 minutes
Oven: 190°C, 375°F, Gas Mark 5

1. Cook the rice in boiling salted water for about 10 minutes or until just tender. Drain and rinse with hot water.
2. Heat the oil in a frying pan, add the onion and fry until lightly coloured. Stir in the tomatoes, beef and mushrooms and cook for a further 5 minutes.
3. Stir in the tomato purée, oregano, rice, salt and pepper. Cool.
4. Put into an ovenproof dish, sprinkle the cheese on top and cook in a preheated oven for about 40 minutes or until heated through.
5. Finish under the grill to brown the cheese. Garnish and serve, with a green salad.

Serves 4

Nutrition content per serving   Carbohydrate: 25g   Fat: 14g
Fibre: 2g   Kilocalories: 316

OXTAIL CASSEROLE

1 good-sized oxtail, trimmed of excess fat and cut into serving pieces
50g (2oz) plain flour
salt
freshly ground black pepper
50g (2oz) lard or dripping
2 onions, peeled and sliced
2 carrots, peeled and sliced
2 celery sticks, diced
450ml (¾ pint) beef stock
1 teaspoon dried mixed herbs
1 bay leaf
juice of ½ lemon

Preparation time: 30 minutes
Cooking time: about 3 hours
Oven: 190°C, 375°F, Gas Mark 5; then 150°C, 300°F, Gas Mark 2

1. Toss the oxtail pieces in the flour seasoned with salt and pepper and reserve any flour left over. Heat the lard or dripping in a large saucepan and fry the oxtail in the hot fat until golden brown. Remove and place it in a casserole.
2. Add the onions, carrots and celery to the pan and cook for 2 minutes. Sprinkle in any leftover flour and stir constantly until the flour browns. Gradually stir in the stock, herbs, bay leaf and lemon juice and bring to the boil, stirring constantly. Season to taste and pour over the oxtail.
3. Cover the casserole and cook in a preheated oven for 30 minutes, then reduce the heat and cook for a further 2 hours or until the oxtail is very tender.

Serves 4

Nutrition content per serving   Carbohydrate: 15g   Fat: 48g
Fibre: 3g   Kilocalories: 778

TOP: Spanish Rice; BOTTOM: Oxtail Casserole.

BEEF & HORSERADISH CREAM

750g (1½ lb) braising steak, cut into 4 portions
salt
freshly ground black pepper
1 teaspoon ground coriander
1 teaspoon ground ginger
2 tablespoons oil or dripping
16 pickling onions, peeled
3 celery sticks, sliced
25g (1oz) plain flour
600ml (1 pint) beef stock
1 tablespoon Worcestershire sauce
2 tablespoons double cream
3–4 tablespoons creamed horseradish
celery leaves, to garnish

Preparation time: 15 minutes
Cooking time: 2½ hours
Oven: 160°C, 325°F, Gas Mark 3

1. Sprinkle the meat with salt and pepper and rub in with the coriander and ginger. Heat the oil in a pan and fry the meat until sealed all over, then place in a shallow casserole.
2. Fry the onions until brown and celery until soft in the same fat. Stir in the flour, cook for 1 minute, then add the stock and bring to the boil. Add salt, pepper and the Worcestershire sauce and pour over the beef. Cover and cook in a preheated oven for 2 hours.
3. Stir in the cream and the horseradish and return to the oven to cook for a further 45 minutes. Serve garnished with celery leaves.

Serves 4

Nutrition content per serving   Carbohydrate: 8g   Fat: 29g
Fibre: 1g   Kilocalories: 435

AUSTRALIAN CURRY HOTPOT

3 tablespoons vegetable oil or dripping
1kg (2lb) braising steak, cut into 2.5cm (1 inch)
*   cubes*
2 large onions, peeled and sliced
2 large cooking apples, peeled, cored and sliced
1 tablespoon curry powder
1 tablespoon plain flour
300ml (½ pint) beef stock
1 × 425g (15oz) can tomatoes
100g (4oz) raisins
2 tablespoons wine vinegar
salt
TO GARNISH:
parsley or coriander sprigs
potato crisps

Preparation time: 15 minutes
Cooking time: 2–2½ hours
Oven: 180°C, 350°F, Gas Mark 4

1. Heat the oil or dripping in a pan and fry the beef until brown. Transfer to a casserole.
2. Fry the onions in the same pan until soft, then add the apples and continue cooking for 2–3 minutes.
3. Sprinkle the curry powder and flour over the onions, mix well, then add the stock and bring to the boil.
4. Add the tomatoes, raisins, vinegar and salt and pour over the beef. Cover the casserole.
5. Cook in a preheated oven for 2 hours. Stir well, adjust the seasoning and if necessary return to the oven to cook for a further 15–30 minutes or until the meat is very tender.
6. Serve garnished with sprigs of parsley or coriander and crisps around the edge.

Serves 5

Nutrition content per serving   Carbohydrate: 30g   Fat: 22g
Fibre: 5g   Kilocalories: 478

LEFT: Beef & Horseradish Cream.
RIGHT: Australian Curry Hotpot.

VEAL & MADEIRA CASSEROLE

25g (1oz) butter
750g (1½ lb) pie veal, cubed
175g (6oz) button onions, peeled
225g (8oz) carrots, peeled and diced
1 small red pepper, seeded and sliced
2 tablespoons plain flour
450ml (¾ pint) chicken stock
4 tablespoons Madeira
salt
freshly ground black pepper
100g (4oz) mushrooms, sliced
2 bay leaves

Preparation time: 20 minutes
Cooking time: 1¼–1½ hours
Oven: 180°C, 350°F, Gas Mark 4

1. Heat the butter in a pan and fry the veal until browned. Transfer to a casserole.
2. Fry the onions and carrots for a few minutes in the same fat until beginning to brown, then add the pepper and cook for 2 minutes.
3. Stir in the flour and cook for 1 minute, then gradually add the stock and Madeira and bring to the boil. Add plenty of salt and pepper, the mushrooms and bay leaves. Pour over the veal.
4. Cover the casserole tightly and cook in a preheated oven for 1¼–1½ hours until tender.

Serves 4

Nutrition content per serving   Carbohydrate: 12g   Fat: 14g
Fibre: 3g   Kilocalories: 354

LEFT: Veal & Madeira Casserole. BELOW: Roman Pie.

ROMAN PIE

1kg (2lb) potatoes, peeled and freshly boiled
2 eggs, beaten
50g (2oz) Parmesan cheese, grated
salt
freshly ground black pepper
2 tablespoons chopped fresh parsley
½ nutmeg, grated
1kg (2lb) minced beef
2 garlic cloves, peeled and crushed
4 tablespoons cold water
25g (1oz) seasoned flour
2–3 tablespoons oil
225g (8oz) mature Cheddar cheese, grated
TOMATO SAUCE:
1 × 225g (8oz) can tomatoes, drained and chopped
½ small onion, peeled and chopped
1 garlic clove, peeled and crushed
½ teaspoon dried basil
a pinch of sugar
2 streaky bacon rashers, rind removed, diced
TO GARNISH:
sautéed sliced courgettes
very thin onion rings

Preparation time: 1¼ hours
Cooking time: 1½ hours
Oven: 180°C, 350°F, Gas Mark 4

1. To make the tomato sauce, put the ingredients in a saucepan and bring to the boil. Cover and simmer gently until thick.
2. Rub the tomato sauce through a sieve and season to taste with salt and pepper.
3. Mash the potatoes and beat in the eggs and Parmesan cheese. Season, then mix in the parsley and nutmeg. Cover and reserve.
4. Mix together the beef, garlic and cold water, working it thoroughly with a wet hand. Season well with salt and pepper. Form into small balls and coat them in the seasoned flour.
5. Heat the oil in a large frying pan, add the beef balls a few at a time and brown all over.
6. Layer the potato, beef balls, tomato sauce and all but 50g (2oz) of the Cheddar cheese into a large casserole, finishing with potato. Cover and cook in a preheated oven for 45 minutes.
7. Remove the lid and sprinkle with the reserved cheese. Cook, uncovered, for 10–15 minutes or until golden brown. Garnish and serve.

Serves 6

Nutrition content per serving   Carbohydrate: 41g   Fat: 53g
Fibre: 4g   Kilocalories: 837

PAPRIKA BEEF

40g (1½ oz) butter
750g (1½ lb) stewing steak, trimmed of excess fat
    and cubed
1 onion, peeled and sliced
1 garlic clove, peeled and crushed
1 tablespoon paprika
2 teaspoons tomato purée
25g (1oz) plain flour
450ml (¾ pint) beef stock
salt
freshly ground black pepper
bouquet garni
½ green pepper, seeded and sliced
2 tomatoes, skinned and quartered
150ml (¼ pint) soured cream

Preparation time: 20 minutes
Cooking time: 3 hours
Oven: 150°C, 300°F, Gas Mark 2

1. Heat 25g (1oz) of the butter and fry the meat lightly on all sides. Remove, drain on paper towels and place in a casserole.
2. Heat the rest of the butter, fry the onion and garlic lightly, then stir in the paprika, tomato purée and flour. Cook for a minute, then slowly add the beef stock.
3. Bring to the boil, stirring all the time, then season well, add the bouquet garni and pour over the meat in the casserole.
4. Cover and cook in a preheated oven for about 2 hours.
5. Add the pepper and tomatoes and cook for a further 30 minutes.
6. Just before serving swirl in the soured cream, and taste and adjust the seasoning. Serve with a green salad and rice or buttered potatoes.

Serves 4

Nutrition content per serving   Carbohydrate: 9g   Fat: 35g
Fibre: 1g   Kilocalories: 505

SIMPLE BEEF CASSEROLE

3 tablespoons oil
750g (1¼ lb) stewing steak, trimmed of excess fat
    and cut into 2.5cm (1 inch) cubes
2 leeks, trimmed, washed and thickly sliced
2 carrots, peeled and sliced
1 large onion, peeled and sliced
25g (1oz) plain flour
450ml (¾ pint) beef stock
1 × 400g (14oz) can tomatoes
salt
freshly ground black pepper

Preparation time: 20 minutes
Cooking time: 3 hours
Oven: 150°C, 300°F, Gas Mark 2

1. Heat the oil in a frying pan and fry the meat briskly on all sides. Remove, drain and place in a casserole. Add the leeks and carrots to the meat.
2. Reheat the remaining oil in the pan and fry the onion until soft. Sprinkle the flour into the pan and cook for 1 minute. Allow to cool slightly, then pour in the stock gradually. Bring to the boil, stirring constantly.
3. Add the tomatoes and season well. Pour the tomato onion sauce into the casserole.
4. Cover and cook in a preheated oven for about 2½ hours. Serve with baked potatoes and French beans.

Serves 4

Nutrition content per serving   Carbohydrate: 15g   Fat: 20g
Fibre: 5g   Kilocalories: 395

TOP: Paprika Beef.
BOTTOM: Simple Beef Casserole.

Lamb

♦

CASSEROLES

Succulent, tender lamb makes wonderful casseroles. Suitable cuts include cubes of boneless shoulder and leg, lamb fillet, best end of neck chops, cutlets and minced lamb.

The recipes in this chapter have an international flavour: Moroccan (apricots, almonds and ginger), Greek (aubergines and allspice), Chinese (bamboo shoots, water chestnuts and soy sauce), South African (apple, raisins and curry powder), French (asparagus and cream) and even Hawaiian (lime, pineapple, cinnamon and cloves). In addition, there are casseroles combining lamb with sweet cider and honey, with fresh ginger and hot spices, and with lentils and a thatched potato topping.

Spiced Lamb with Orange Rice (see recipe on page 24).

SPICED LAMB WITH ORANGE RICE

3 large onions, peeled and grated or minced
2 bay leaves, very finely crumbled
100g (4oz) butter
6 tablespoons water
750g (1½ lb) lean lamb, cut into 2.5cm (1 inch)
  cubes
2 garlic cloves, peeled and crushed
1cm (½ inch) piece fresh ginger, peeled and finely
  chopped
1 tablespoon ground coriander
1 teaspoon ground cumin
2 teaspoons paprika
½ teaspoon cayenne (or to taste)
1 teaspoon salt
150ml (¼ pint) plain unsweetened yogurt
225g (8oz) potatoes, peeled and diced
2 teaspoons lemon juice
4 large tomatoes, skinned and quartered
1 lemon, quartered, to serve
ORANGE RICE:
1 tablespoon vegetable oil
225g (8oz) long-grain rice
1 teaspoon ground turmeric
600ml (1 pint) chicken stock or water
1 teaspoon salt
1 orange
2 tablespoons blanched almonds, toasted
parsley sprig, to garnish

Preparation time: 30 minutes
Cooking time: 1¾ hours
Oven: 180°C, 350°F, Gas Mark 4

1. Fry the onions and bay leaves in half the butter over moderate heat for 8–10 minutes, stirring frequently, until they are medium brown, but not burning. Stir in 1 tablespoon of the water until it forms a paste. Transfer the onions to a casserole.
2. Fry the lamb in the remaining butter for about 3 minutes on each side, until it is sealed. Transfer the meat to the casserole.
3. Fry the garlic and ginger in the fat remaining in the pan for 2 minutes, then stir in the spices and cook for 1 minute. Stir in the remaining water, salt and yogurt, and bring the sauce slowly to the boil. Add to the casserole.
4. Cover the casserole and cook in a preheated oven for 30 minutes. Add the potatoes and lemon juice and cook for a further 45 minutes.
5. About 30 minutes before the lamb dish is ready, start cooking the orange rice. Heat the vegetable oil in a pan and stir the rice over

moderate heat for 1 minute. Stir in the turmeric, then add the stock or water, and the salt. Cover the pan and simmer for 15 minutes, or until the rice is just tender.
6. Meanwhile, grate the orange rind. Peel the orange and divide the flesh into segments.
7. Remove the pan from the heat and leave the rice to rest for 5 minutes, then stir in the orange rind and segments and most of the almonds. Garnish the rice with the remaining almonds and the parsley.
8. Add the tomatoes to the lamb casserole and cook for a further 5 minutes. Serve with the rice and lemon wedges.

Serves 4

Nutrition content per serving   Carbohydrate: 71g   Fat: 45g
Fibre: 6g   Kilocalories: 929

COUNTRY LAMB CASSEROLE

1kg (2lb) best end of neck of lamb
salt
freshly ground black pepper
225g (8oz) onions, peeled and sliced
450g (1lb) carrots, peeled and chopped
750g (1½ lb) potatoes, peeled and thickly sliced
½ teaspoon dried thyme
900ml (1½ pints) boiling water
chopped fresh parsley, to garnish

Preparation time: 15 minutes
Cooking time: 2 hours
Oven: 160°C, 325°F, Gas Mark 3

1. Cut neck into chops and season well. Put alternate layers of vegetables and meat in a large casserole, finishing with a layer of potato. Season well between the layers and sprinkle in the herbs at the same time.
2. Pour the water over the top, cover and cook in a preheated oven for about 2 hours.
3. Just before serving, skim well and sprinkle with parsley. Serve with buttered cabbage.

Serves 4

Nutrition content per serving   Carbohydrate: 45g   Fat: 87g
Fibre: 7g   Kilocalories: 1133

Country Lamb Casserole.

LAMB & LENTIL HOTPOT

*275g (10oz) brown continental lentils, soaked for
  1–2 hours and drained*
1 bay leaf
2–3 tablespoons vegetable oil
*1kg (2¼ lb) lean lamb, trimmed of excess fat and
  thickly sliced*
1 large onion, peeled and sliced
4 spring onions, trimmed and sliced
2 garlic cloves, peeled and chopped
350g (12oz) tomatoes, skinned and sliced
150ml (¼ pint) chicken stock
salt
freshly ground black pepper
a pinch of ground coriander
2 tablespoons chopped fresh parsley
450g (1lb) potatoes, peeled and thinly sliced

Preparation time: 20 minutes plus soaking
Cooking time: 2 hours
Oven: 180°C, 350°F, Gas Mark 4

1. Put the lentils into a saucepan, cover with
water and add the bay leaf. Bring to the boil
and simmer for 15 minutes. Drain the lentils in
a colander.
2. Heat the oil in a flameproof casserole and
fry the slices of lamb for 3 minutes on each
side until they are evenly browned.
3. Lift out the meat with a draining spoon. Fry
the onions and garlic in the casserole over
moderate heat for 3 minutes, stirring once or
twice. Add the lentils, tomatoes and stock and
bring to the boil. Season with salt, pepper and
coriander and stir in the parsley. Mix in the
lamb. Place the potato slices on top and cover
the casserole.
4. Cook in a preheated oven for 1¼ hours.
Remove the lid and continue cooking for 30
minutes to brown the potatoes.
5. Serve hot with a green vegetable.

Serves 6

Nutrition content per serving   Carbohydrate: 42g   Fat: 19g
Fibre: 8g   Kilocalories: 506

BOBOTIE

Bobotie is one of South Africa's typical
informal dishes, although Malay in origin, and
on par in popularity with our Shepherd's pie.
It consists of curried minced lamb with a
savoury custard topping. Bobotie is the perfect
cook ahead dish since it needs little last minute
attention.

25g (1oz) butter
1 onion, peeled and finely chopped
1 dessert apple, peeled, cored and finely chopped
1 tablespoon mild curry powder
1 tablespoon apricot jam or mango chutney
1 large slice bread, crusts removed
300ml (½ pint) milk
750g (1½ lb) lean minced cooked lamb
25g (1oz) seedless raisins
1 tablespoon lemon juice
salt
freshly ground black pepper
2 eggs, beaten
few lemon, lime, orange or bay leaves
25g (1oz) flaked almonds

Preparation time: 20 minutes
Cooking time: 55 minutes
Oven: 180°C, 350°F, Gas Mark 4

1. Melt the butter in a pan. Add the onion and
apple and cook for about 5 minutes until
softened.
2. Add the curry powder and cook for 2
minutes. Stir in the jam or chutney and cook
for a further 1 minute. Remove from the heat.
3. Meanwhile, soak the bread in 2–3
tablespoons of the milk. Squeeze to remove any
excess moisture then mix with the lamb, onion
mixture, raisins, lemon juice and salt and
pepper to taste. Place in a 1.5 litre (2½ pint)
shallow ovenproof dish and smooth the surface.
4. Beat the eggs with the remaining milk and
salt and pepper to taste. Strain over the top of
the meat mixture. Top with the leaves and
scatter with the almonds.
5. Place in a preheated oven and cook for 45
minutes or until the topping is set and golden.
Serve hot with fluffy boiled rice, sliced onion,
tomatoes, chutney and poppadums.

Serves 4

Nutrition content per serving   Carbohydrate: 19g   Fat: 30g
Fibre: 2g   Kilocalories: 594

TOP: Bobotie; BOTTOM: Lamb & Lentil Hotpot.

MOUSSAKA

2 medium-sized aubergines, about 450g (1lb)
  total, sliced, sprinkled with salt and drained
about 120ml (4fl oz) olive or other vegetable oil
1 large onion, peeled and chopped
1 garlic clove, peeled and crushed
450g (1lb) cooked lamb, minced
1 teaspoon ground allspice or cinnamon
2 tablespoons chopped fresh parsley
freshly ground black pepper
3 tablespoons tomato purée
450g (1lb) potatoes, parboiled, peeled and thinly
  sliced
SAUCE:
25g (1oz) butter
40g (1½ oz) plain flour
450ml (¾ pint) hot milk
a pinch of ground allspice
salt
freshly ground black pepper
1 egg yolk

Preparation time: 45 minutes
Cooking time: about 1¼ hours
Oven: 190°C, 375°F, Gas Mark 5

1. Dry the aubergines thoroughly on a clean
tea-towel or paper towels. Heat 3 tablespoons
oil in a large frying pan and add enough
aubergine slices to cover the bottom of the pan.
Fry until browned on both sides. Remove from
the pan with a slotted spoon and drain on
paper towels.
2. Fry the remaining aubergine slices in this
way, adding more oil when necessary.
3. Fry the onion and garlic until golden in the
same pan. Stir in the lamb and fry until
browned. Add the allspice or cinnamon,
parsley, and pepper to taste, then stir in the
tomato purée and a little water to moisten.
4. In a large casserole or earthenware cooking
pot, put alternate layers of meat and
aubergines, starting and ending with a meat
layer. Put a layer of potatoes on top of this.
5. To prepare the sauce, melt the butter in a
saucepan. Stir in the flour and cook for 1–2
minutes, stirring constantly. Remove from the
heat and gradually add the hot milk, stirring
vigorously. When all the milk is incorporated,
return to the heat and bring to the boil, stirring
constantly. Lower the heat, add the seasonings
and simmer gently until the sauce thickens.
Remove from the heat and allow to cool
slightly. Beat the egg yolk in a mixing bowl

then beat a few spoons of the sauce into the
egg. Stir this mixture into the pan of sauce and
taste for seasoning. Spoon the sauce over the
potatoes in the baking dish.
6. Bake in a preheated oven for 25–30 minutes
when the sauce topping will have risen and
become golden. Remove from the oven, allow
to cool for a few minutes, then serve straight
from the cooking dish.

Serves 4

Nutrition content per serving   Carbohydrate: 44g   Fat: 51g
Fibre: 6g   Kilocalories: 796

HONEYED LAMB

750g (1½ lb) lean lamb, cut from the leg
2 medium onions, peeled and sliced
2 medium carrots, peeled and sliced
2 celery sticks, thinly sliced
½ teaspoon dried thyme
120ml (4fl oz) sweet cider
2 tablespoons clear honey
1 tablespoon red wine vinegar
salt
freshly ground black pepper
7.5g (¼ oz) butter
1 teaspoon plain flour

Preparation time: 30 minutes
Cooking time: 55 minutes
Oven: 200°C, 400°F, Gas Mark 6

1. Cut the meat into 2.5cm (1 inch) cubes and
trim off any fat. Put the onions, carrots and
celery into a casserole and add the meat in a
single layer. Sprinkle on the thyme.
2. Heat the cider and honey. When the honey
has melted, stir in the vinegar and pour the
sauce over the meat. Add salt and pepper to
taste.
3. Cover and cook in a preheated oven for 45
minutes.
4. Beat together the butter and flour, stir into
the casserole and return to the oven to cook for
5 minutes. Taste and adjust the seasoning.

Serves 4

Nutrition content per serving   Carbohydrate: 15g   Fat: 18g
Fibre: 3g   Kilocalories: 389

TOP: Moussaka; BOTTOM: Honeyed Lamb.

LAMB CASSEROLED WITH LIME

2 onions, peeled and sliced
3 tablespoons vegetable oil
750g (1½ lb) lamb fillet, cubed
a pinch of ground cinnamon
a pinch of ground cloves
2 tablespoons plain flour
300ml (½ pint) pineapple juice
300ml (½ pint) chicken stock
3 limes or 2 lemons
fresh mint or rosemary sprigs, to garnish
(optional)

Preparation time: 25 minutes
Cooking time: 1¼ hours
Oven: 180°C, 350°F, Gas Mark 4

1. Fry the onions gently in the oil in a flameproof casserole for 3 minutes. Add the cubed lamb and cook over moderate heat until lightly browned on all sides.
2. Stir in the cinnamon, cloves and flour and cook for 1 minute. Gradually stir in the pineapple juice and chicken stock. Squeeze the juice from 2 of the limes (or 1½ lemons) and add to the pan.
3. Cover and transfer to a preheated oven. Cook for 1 hour.
4. Serve garnished with thin slices of the remaining lime or ½ lemon, and small sprigs of mint, if liked.

Serves 4

Nutrition content per serving   Carbohydrate: 19g   Fat: 24g
Fibre: 1g   Kilocalories: 449

LAMB WITH ASPARAGUS SAUCE

You will need a 2kg (4lb) shoulder of lamb in order to have 1kg (2lb) boneless meat. Ask the butcher to bone it for you as it can be a time-consuming task.

25g (1oz) butter
1 medium onion, peeled and thinly sliced
1–2 garlic cloves, peeled and crushed
1kg (2lb) boneless shoulder of lamb, trimmed of
*   fat and cut into cubes*
juice of 1 lemon
300ml (½ pint) chicken stock
freshly ground black pepper
1 × 225g (8oz) packet frozen asparagus spears,
*   thawed*
salt
150ml (¼ pint) double cream, to finish

Preparation time: 15 minutes
Cooking time: 2–2½ hours
Oven: 160°C, 325°F, Gas Mark 3

1. Melt the butter in a large flameproof casserole, add the onion and fry gently until soft. Add the garlic and lamb and fry over moderate heat until the lamb is lightly browned on all sides.
2. Stir the lemon juice into the casserole, together with the stock and pepper to taste. Bring to the boil, then lower the heat and simmer gently for 5 minutes.
3. Trim the tips off the asparagus spears and reserve. Stir the spears into the lamb mixture, then cover and transfer to a preheated oven. Cook for 1½–2 hours or until the lamb is tender, stirring occasionally.
4. Meanwhile cook the reserved asparagus tips in simmering water for 3–5 minutes. Drain and set aside.
5. Return the casserole to the top of the stove and spoon away any fat from the surface. Taste and adjust the seasoning of the sauce. Mix together the cream and reserved asparagus tips, then pour carefully over the surface of the casserole in a thin, even layer. Heat through gently without stirring.

Serves 4

Nutrition content per serving   Carbohydrate: 3g   Fat: 45g
Fibre: 1g   Kilocalories: 636

TOP: Lamb Casseroled with Lime; BOTTOM: Lamb with Asparagus Sauce.

CHINESE LAMB CUTLETS

8 lamb cutlets
50g (2oz) seasoned flour
2 tablespoons vegetable oil
1 onion, peeled and chopped
450ml (¾ pint) stock
1 × 200g (7oz) can bamboo shoots, drained and
   sliced
100g (4oz) mushrooms, sliced
1 × 200g (7oz) can water chestnuts, drained and
   sliced
2 celery sticks, sliced
2 tablespoons soy sauce
salt
freshly ground black pepper
spring onion greens, to garnish
FRIED RICE:
2 spring onions, finely chopped
3 eggs, beaten
1 teaspoon salt
4 tablespoons vegetable oil
50g (2oz) cooked ham, diced
100g (4oz) peas, cooked
175g (6oz) long-grain rice, cooked
1 tablespoon soy sauce

Preparation time: 40 minutes
Cooking time: 45 minutes
Oven: 180°C, 350°F, Gas Mark 4

1. Coat the cutlets with the seasoned flour.
2. Heat the oil in a large frying pan, add the
cutlets and brown well on each side. Transfer
them to a casserole.
3. Add the onion to the frying pan and cook
until golden. Stir in any remaining seasoned
flour and cook for 2 minutes.
4. Stir in the stock and bring to the boil. Put
the bamboo shoots, mushrooms, water
chestnuts and celery into the casserole.
5. Add the soy sauce to the stock mixture,
season to taste with salt and pepper and pour
into the casserole.
6. Cover and cook in a preheated oven for 45
minutes or until the lamb is tender.
7. Meanwhile, make the fried rice. Mix half
the spring onions with the eggs and a pinch of
salt.
8. Heat a third of the oil in a frying pan, then
add the eggs and stir until scrambled. Transfer
to a warm plate and break up with a fork.
9. Heat the remaining oil in the pan. Add the
remaining spring onions, the ham, peas, rice
and soy sauce. Stir over the heat until hot.

10. Add the eggs, reduce the heat and cook for
a further minute.
11. Garnish the lamb with spring onion greens
and serve with the fried rice and soy sauce.

Serves 4

Nutrition content per serving   Carbohydrate: 62g   Fat: 77g
Fibre: 7g   Kilocalories: 1077

MOROCCAN LAMB

2 tablespoons oil
1 large onion, peeled and thinly sliced
1 garlic clove, peeled and crushed
1.5kg (3lb) boned shoulder of lamb, cubed
1 × 400g (14oz) can apricot halves
50g (2oz) blanched almonds
½ teaspoon ground ginger
2 tablespoons tomato purée
300ml (½ pint) hot beef stock
salt
freshly ground black pepper
1 tablespoon cornflour
1½ tablespoons cold water

Preparation time: 30 minutes
Cooking time: 1½–2 hours
Oven: 180°C, 350°F, Gas Mark 4

1. Heat the oil in a frying pan. Add the onion
and garlic and fry until the onion is soft.
Transfer to a casserole, draining well.
2. Add the lamb cubes to the frying pan and
brown on all sides. Transfer to the casserole.
Drain the apricots, reserving the juice, and add
to the casserole with the almonds.
3. Mix together the reserved apricot juice,
ginger, tomato purée and hot stock. Add to the
casserole with a little salt and pepper and stir.
4. Cover and cook in a preheated oven for 1–1½
hours or until the lamb is very tender.
5. Before serving, dissolve the cornflour in the
cold water and stir into the lamb stew until
thickened. Taste and adjust the seasoning.

Serves 8

Nutrition content per serving   Carbohydrate: 17g   Fat: 24g
Fibre: 2g   Kilocalories: 438

TOP: Moroccan Lamb; BOTTOM: Chinese Lamb
Cutlets.

Pork
◆
CASSEROLES

A casserole based on pork can be simple or special, according to the occasion. In this chapter you will find many casseroles suitable for family suppers – a hotpot with apples and sage topped with mashed potato, cubes of pork with lots of vegetables finished with a layer of grated Cheddar, a bake of pork and beans in a sweet and sour sauce, and sausages casseroled with tomato rice and bacon.

For more special suppers, you might like to try tender pieces of pork and prunes in a creamy white wine sauce, or pork with orange segments and walnuts in a cinnamon-spiced orange cream sauce.

There are some unusual casseroles, too, such as the traditional American dish Jambalaya – strips of pork and smoked pork sausage cooked in a spicy rice mixture with green and red peppers and prawns – and an Indian vindaloo-style dish, spicy but not too hot.

Pork & Apple Hotpot (see recipe on page 36).

PORK & APPLE HOTPOT

Substantial and nourishing, pork and apple
hotpot would make a good family supper dish.
Serve it straight from the casserole with a
seasonal green vegetable.

750g (1½ lb) lean boneless pork, cut into cubes
1 teaspoon dry English mustard
1 teaspoon chopped fresh sage, or ½ teaspoon
*   dried sage*
salt
freshly ground black pepper
1 large onion, peeled and finely chopped
2 large cooking apples, peeled, cored and sliced,
*   and soaked in water mixed with juice of*
*   ½ lemon*
4 tablespoons cider or water
4 large potatoes, boiled and mashed with
*   25g (1oz) butter, 2 tablespoons milk and*
*   1 beaten egg*
25g (1oz) butter

Preparation time: 1 hour
Cooking time: 1½–2 hours
Oven: 180°C, 350°F, Gas Mark 4

1. Put the pork in a large casserole and mix in
the mustard, sage, and salt and pepper to taste.
Add the onion and drained apple slices and stir
well to mix.
2. Pour over the cider or water, cover the
casserole and cook in a preheated oven for 1½–2
hours, depending on the cut of pork, or until
the meat is very tender.
3. About 20 minutes before the end of the
cooking time, remove the lid, taste for
seasoning and spread the mashed potatoes over
the top of the casserole. Dot with butter,
return to the oven and cook until golden.

Serves 4

Nutrition content per serving   Carbohydrate: 53g   Fat: 21g
Fibre: 7g   Kilocalories: 569

PORK WITH PRUNES & WHITE WINE

16 prunes
300ml (½ pint) dry white wine
50g (2oz) butter
750g (1½ lb) pork fillet, cut into bite-sized pieces
salt
freshly ground black pepper
2 tablespoons redcurrant jelly
1 teaspoon lemon juice
150ml (¼ pint) double cream

Preparation time: 15 minutes, plus soaking
Cooking time: 50 minutes
Oven: 180°C, 350°F, Gas Mark 4

1. Put the prunes in a shallow bowl, pour in
the wine, cover and soak overnight.
2. Drain the prunes, reserving the liquid, and
remove the stones.
3. Melt the butter in a flameproof casserole,
add the pork and cook over brisk heat until
lightly coloured on all sides. Sprinkle with salt
and pepper. Add the prunes, pour over the
reserved liquid and bring to the boil. Cover
and cook in a preheated oven for 30 minutes or
until the pork is tender.
4. Remove the pork and prunes from the pan
with a slotted spoon and place on a warmed
serving platter. Keep hot.
5. Add the redcurrant jelly and lemon juice to
the pan and stir until the jelly has melted. Stir
in the cream and bring to the boil. Continue
boiling for 5–10 minutes until the sauce is
thickened and just beginning to turn golden,
whisking continuously with a wire balloon
whisk.
6. Taste and adjust the seasoning, then pour
over the pork. Serve immediately.

Serves 4

Nutrition content per serving   Carbohydrate: 28g   Fat: 42g
Fibre: 8g   Kilocalories: 690

Pork with Prunes & White Wine.

CHEESY PORK POT

2 tablespoons oil
1 onion, peeled and sliced
450g (1lb) pork fillet, cubed
1 × 400g (14oz) can tomatoes
4 small leeks, cleaned and sliced
4 small courgettes, sliced
1 teaspoon finely chopped fresh basil
salt
freshly ground black pepper
450g (1lb) potatoes, peeled and sliced
100g (4oz) Cheddar cheese, grated
fresh basil sprig, to garnish

Preparation time: 20 minutes
Cooking time: 1 hour
Oven: 180°C, 350°F, Gas Mark 4

1. Heat the oil in a flameproof casserole. Add the onion and pork and brown on all sides for about 10 minutes.
2. Add the tomatoes, leeks, courgettes, basil and salt and pepper to taste, blending well. Remove from the heat and layer the potatoes on top of the meat and vegetable mixture.
3. Place, covered, in a preheated oven and cook for 30 minutes.
4. Sprinkle with the cheese and bake, uncovered, for a further 20 minutes. Serve garnished with a basil sprig.

Serves 4

Nutrition content per serving   Carbohydrate: 33g   Fat: 24g
Fibre: 6g   Kilocalories: 484

COUNTRY PORK CASSEROLE

450g (1lb) pork fillet, trimmed of excess fat and cut into slices
50g (2oz) plain flour
salt
freshly ground black pepper
50g (2oz) butter
2 onions, peeled and sliced
1 large leek, trimmed, washed and sliced
100g (4oz) celery, scrubbed, trimmed and diced
1 small green pepper, seeded and sliced
225g (8oz) tomatoes, skinned, seeded and chopped
1 tablespoon white wine vinegar
150ml ($\frac{1}{4}$ pint) tomato juice

Preparation time: 45 minutes
Cooking time: 1 hour–1 hour 10 minutes
Oven: 180°C, 350°F, Gas Mark 4

1. Coat the pork slices in the flour seasoned with salt and pepper. Heat the butter in a frying pan and fry the pork on either side until golden brown. Remove to a casserole.
2. Add the onion, leek and celery to the pan and fry for 10 minutes, then spoon on to the pork, together with the green pepper and tomatoes. Season to taste and pour over the vinegar and tomato juice.
3. Cover the casserole and bake in a preheated oven for 40–50 minutes or until just tender.

Serves 4

Nutrition content per serving   Carbohydrate: 18g   Fat: 18g
Fibre: 3g   Kilocalories: 339

LEFT: Cheesy Pork Pot.
ABOVE: Country Pork Casserole.

PORK VINDALOO-STYLE

1 tablespoon coriander seeds
1 tablespoon cumin seeds
1 tablespoon sesame seeds
4 cloves
3 tablespoons vegetable oil
750g (1½ lb) pork fillet, cubed
1 tablespoon turmeric
2 tablespoons soft brown sugar
150ml (¼ pint) wine vinegar
150ml (¼ pint) chicken stock or water
salt
freshly ground black pepper
TO SERVE:
chopped onion
chopped green pepper
tomato slices
rice
plain unsweetened yogurt

Preparation time: 15 minutes
Cooking time: 1¾ hours
Oven: 180°C, 350°F, Gas Mark 4

1. Fry the coriander seeds, cumin seeds, sesame seeds and cloves in the oil in a flameproof casserole for 2 minutes. Add the cubed pork fillet and fry over moderate heat until lightly browned on all sides. Add the turmeric and cook for 1 minute.
2. Stir in the brown sugar, vinegar, stock or water, and salt and pepper. Cover and cook in a preheated oven for 1½ hours. There should not be very much juice with this dish, but if it becomes too dry during cooking add a little extra stock or water.
3. Transfer to a flat serving dish, and serve with dishes of chopped onion, chopped green pepper, tomato slices, cooked rice and a bowl of chilled yogurt.

Serves 4

Nutrition content per serving   Carbohydrate: 10g   Fat: 31g
Fibre: 0g   Kilocalories: 473

BRAISED PORK IN ORANGE SAUCE

2 medium onions, peeled and chopped
3 tablespoons oil
600g (1¼ lb) pork fillet, cubed
seasoned flour
300ml (½ pint) unsweetened orange juice
150ml (¼ pint) chicken stock
225g (8oz) carrots, peeled and grated
a pinch of ground cinnamon
salt
freshly ground black pepper
2 oranges, peel and pith removed, cut into
    segments
150ml (¼ pint) double cream
2 tablespoons chopped walnuts
fresh mint sprigs, to garnish

Preparation time: 30 minutes
Cooking time: 1½ hours
Oven: 180°C, 350°F, Gas Mark 4

1. Fry the chopped onion in the oil in a flameproof casserole for 3 minutes over low heat. Dust the cubed pork in seasoned flour and add to the onion. Cook over moderate heat until the meat is lightly browned on all sides.
2. Gradually stir in the orange juice and chicken stock. Bring to the boil and add the carrots, cinnamon, and salt and pepper. Cover and cook in a preheated oven for 30 minutes.
3. Stir in the orange segments (reserving a few for garnish, if liked), double cream and walnuts. Return to the oven and cook for a further 40 minutes. Serve hot, garnished with mint sprigs.

Serves 4

Nutrition content per serving   Carbohydrate: 20g   Fat: 44g
Fibre: 4g   Kilocalories: 610

TOP: Pork Vindaloo-Style; BOTTOM: Braised Pork in Orange Sauce.

BACON & SAUSAGE SPECIAL

100g (4oz) long-grain rice
salt
2 teaspoons oil
450g (1lb) pork or turkey sausages
50g (2oz) butter
2 onions, peeled and finely chopped
300ml ($\frac{1}{2}$ pint) canned or bottled tomato juice
2 fresh basil sprigs, finely chopped, or 1 bay leaf
freshly ground black pepper
4 tomatoes, skinned and thickly sliced
8 thin streaky bacon rashers, rind removed
bay leaves or parsley sprigs, to garnish

Preparation time: 25 minutes
Cooking time: 55 minutes
Oven: 160 C, 325°F, Gas Mark 3

1. Add the rice to a saucepan of rapidly boiling salted water, then cover and cook for 10 minutes or until barely tender.
2. Meanwhile, heat the oil in a frying pan, add the sausages and brown on all sides.
3. Melt the butter in a flameproof casserole, add the onions and cook gently until softened. Add the drained rice and turn it over to absorb the butter. Stir in the tomato juice, basil or bay leaf and salt and pepper to taste.
4. Bury the sausages in the rice mixture. Top with the tomato slices and season with salt and pepper. Cover and cook in a preheated oven for 40 minutes.
5. Remove the lid and make a lattice with the streaky bacon over the top. Cook, uncovered, for a further 15 minutes or until the topping is crisp.
6. Garnish with bay leaves or parsley sprigs and serve with buttered cabbage.

Serves 4

Nutrition content per serving   Carbohydrate: 37g   Fat: 49g
Fibre: 3g   Kilocalories: 630

SWEET-SOUR PORK & BEAN BAKE

450g (1lb) dried butter beans, soaked in water
    overnight and drained
2 tablespoons oil
450g (1lb) boned pork shoulder, cubed
1 onion, peeled and finely chopped
150ml ($\frac{1}{4}$ pint) tomato ketchup
juice of 1 lemon
1 tablespoon Dijon mustard
1 teaspoon chopped fresh basil, or 1 teaspoon
    dried basil
4 tablespoons white wine vinegar
1 tablespoon soft brown sugar
150ml ($\frac{1}{4}$ pint) hot chicken stock
salt
freshly ground black pepper
flat-leaf parsley sprigs, to garnish (optional)

Preparation time: 20 minutes, plus soaking
Cooking time: 2–2$\frac{1}{2}$ hours
Oven: 160°C, 325°F, Gas Mark 3

1. Put the beans into a saucepan, cover with fresh cold water and bring to the boil. Simmer for 1 hour, then drain.
2. Heat the oil in a large frying pan, add the pork and brown on all sides. Transfer to a deep casserole.
3. Add the onion to the pan and cook gently until softened. Add to the casserole together with the beans, ketchup, lemon juice, mustard, basil, vinegar, brown sugar and stock. Season to taste with salt and pepper and mix well.
4. Cover the casserole and cook in a preheated oven for 1–1$\frac{1}{2}$ hours or until the meat is tender and the sauce is the consistency of thick cream.
5. Adjust the seasoning, then turn into a heated serving dish. Garnish with parsley sprigs, if liked.

Serves 6

Nutrition content per serving   Carbohydrate: 47g   Fat: 12g
Fibre: 16g   Kilocalories: 410

TOP: Bacon & Sausage Special; BOTTOM: Sweet-Sour Pork & Bean Bake.

JAMBALAYA

2 tablespoons oil
25g (1oz) butter
450g (1lb) boneless pork, cut into narrow strips
1 large onion, peeled and chopped
1 green pepper, seeded and sliced
1 red pepper, seeded and sliced
100g (4oz) mushrooms, thickly sliced
150g (5oz) long-grain rice
450ml ($\frac{3}{4}$ pint) beef stock
$\frac{1}{4}$ teaspoon ground allspice
salt
freshly ground black pepper
100g (4oz) smoked sausage, sliced or chopped
100g (4oz) peeled prawns
TO GARNISH:
few whole prawns
tomato wedges

Preparation time: 20 minutes
Cooking time: 1 hour
Oven: 180°C, 350°F, Gas Mark 4

1. Heat the oil and butter in a pan and fry the pieces of pork until well browned. Transfer to a large casserole.
2. Fry the onion gently in the same fat until soft. Add the peppers and continue cooking for 3–4 minutes, stirring frequently.
3. Add the mushrooms and continue cooking for a further 1 minute, then stir in the rice followed by the stock and bring to the boil.
4. Add the allspice, salt and pepper and the smoked sausage. Pour over the pork, mix well and cover tightly. Cook in a preheated oven for 45 minutes.

5. Stir well, and add the prawns and a little more boiling stock if necessary. Cover again and return to the oven to cook for about 15 minutes or until the liquid has been absorbed and the meat is tender.
6. Garnish with whole prawns and tomato wedges.

Serves 4

Nutrition content per serving   Carbohydrate: 36g   Fat: 28g
Fibre: 2g   Kilocalories: 527

CIDERED SAUSAGES & KIDNEYS

450g (1lb) chipolata sausages
4 lambs' kidneys, skinned, trimmed and halved
1 onion, peeled and sliced
25g (1oz) plain flour
300ml ($\frac{1}{2}$ pint) dry cider
300ml ($\frac{1}{2}$ pint) beef stock
salt
freshly ground black pepper
2 celery sticks, scrubbed and chopped
2 carrots, peeled and sliced
bouquet garni

Preparation time: 30 minutes
Cooking time: 1$\frac{3}{4}$ hours
Oven: 180°C, 350°F, Gas Mark 4

1. Fry the sausages until lightly browned. Remove from the pan and place in a casserole. Lightly fry the kidneys, then transfer to the casserole.
2. Fry the onion until softened in the remaining fat in the pan. Add the flour and cook for 2 minutes, then gradually pour on the cider and stock. Bring to the boil, stirring. Season well.
3. Put the rest of the vegetables into the casserole and pour over the cider sauce. Add the bouquet garni. Cover and cook in a preheated oven for about 1 hour. Remove bouquet garni before serving, with baked or boiled potatoes.

Serves 4

Nutrition content per serving   Carbohydrate: 22g   Fat: 38g
Fibre: 3g   Kilocalories: 520

LEFT: Jambalaya.
RIGHT: Cidered Sausages & Kidneys.

HAM & POTATO GRATIN

750g (1½ lb) potatoes, peeled and very thinly sliced
225g (8oz) ham sausage, sliced
2 onions, peeled and sliced
175g (6oz) Cheddar cheese, grated
salt
freshly ground black pepper
1 teaspoon grated nutmeg
2 eggs
300ml (½ pint) milk
3 tablespoons double cream
25g (1oz) butter

Preparation time: 15 minutes
Cooking time: 1½ hours
Oven: 160°C, 325°F, Gas Mark 3

1. Fill a medium ovenproof dish with alternate layers of potato, ham sausage, onion and cheese, adding salt, pepper and nutmeg between each layer.
2. Beat the eggs with the milk and cream and pour over the dish. Dot with the butter. Place in a preheated oven and cook for 1½ hours or until heated through and golden brown.
3. Serve at once, straight from the dish. Accompany the dish with a green or mixed salad.

Variations:

Tongue and potato gratin: use 225g (8oz) sliced cooked tongue instead of the ham sausage.
Garlic sausage and potato gratin: use 225g (8oz) sliced garlic sausage instead of the ham sausage.
Bacon and potato gratin: use 225g (8oz) crispy-fried chopped bacon instead of the ham sausage.

Serves 4

Nutrition content per serving   Carbohydrate: 42g   Fat: 46g
Fibre: 4g   Kilocalories: 673

FRANKFURTER RICE WITH GHERKINS

25g (1oz) butter
1 tablespoon vegetable oil
1 large Spanish onion, peeled and chopped
175g (6oz) long-grain rice
300ml (½ pint) chicken stock
50g (2oz) sweetcorn kernels
40g (1½oz) sultanas
225g (8oz) frankfurters, sliced
salt
freshly ground black pepper
TO SERVE:
2 sweet/sour gherkins, sliced
1 hard-boiled egg, chopped

Preparation time: 15 minutes
Cooking time: about 1 hour
Oven: 180°C, 350°F, Gas Mark 4

1. Melt the butter and oil in a saucepan, add the onion and cook gently for 5 minutes until softened but not coloured.
2. Stir in the rice and stock and bring to the boil. Simmer gently for about 25 minutes or until the rice is tender and the stock has been absorbed. Stir occasionally.
3. Add the sweetcorn, sultanas, frankfurters, and salt and pepper to taste.
4. Put into an ovenproof dish, cover and cook in a preheated oven for 30 minutes.
5. Stir in the gherkins and sprinkle with the chopped egg. Serve with a green or tomato salad.

Serves 4

Nutrition content per serving   Carbohydrate: 50g   Fat: 25g
Fibre: 3g   Kilocalories: 456

TOP: Ham & Potato Gratin; BOTTOM: Frankfurter Rice with Gherkins.

Poultry & game

◆

CASSEROLES

Poultry is, without doubt, the most versatile of meats: it can be cooked in so many ways, and lends itself particularly well to casseroling. In addition, it is nutritious and low in saturated fat. The casseroles in this chapter use chicken, turkey and rabbit in very imaginative ways: with apples and cider, in a sweet and sour sauce with pineapple, in an Italian-style tomato, red wine and herb sauce, with a flavouring of treacle, lemon and walnuts, in a deliciously spicy Mexican sauce, and in a hearty dish with two kinds of beans.

In addition, there are some tempting game casseroles: pheasant (with dried apricots and orange), venison (with blackcurrants), guinea fowl (with grapes) and pigeons (with black cherries).

Turkey Mexicana (see recipe on page 50).

TURKEY MEXICANA

Chilli powder is very hot and varies in strength according to the brand, so use it cautiously.

50g (2oz) seasoned flour
4 turkey fillets
3 tablespoons vegetable oil
1 medium onion, peeled and thinly sliced
1 small red pepper, seeded and sliced
300ml ($\frac{1}{2}$ pint) chicken stock
25g (1oz) seedless raisins
a pinch of ground cloves
a pinch of ground cumin
$\frac{1}{2}$ teaspoon ground cinnamon
3 tomatoes, skinned, seeded and sliced
1 teaspoon chilli powder
1 tablespoon sesame seeds
25g (1oz) plain dark chocolate, grated
salt
freshly ground black pepper
parsley sprigs or fresh coriander leaves, to garnish

Preparation time: 20 minutes
Cooking time: 1 hour
Oven: 160°C, 325°F, Gas Mark 3

1. Use the seasoned flour to coat the turkey fillets.
2. Heat the oil in a frying pan, add the turkey and cook until lightly browned. Transfer to a casserole.
3. Add the onion and red pepper to the frying pan and cook gently until they begin to soften. Sprinkle in any remaining seasoned flour and cook for 2–3 minutes.
4. Stir in the stock, raisins, cloves, cumin, cinnamon, tomatoes, chilli powder, sesame seeds and chocolate. Season lightly with salt and pepper. Bring to the boil and simmer for 10 minutes.
5. Pour the sauce over the turkey. Cover the casserole and cook in a preheated oven for 50 minutes. Adjust the seasoning, then garnish with parsley or coriander.
6. Serve with sweetcorn and green beans.

Serves 4

Nutrition content per serving   Carbohydrate: 20g   Fat: 15g
Fibre: 2g   Kilocalories: 334

CHICKEN PAPRIKASH

50g (2oz) plain flour
1$\frac{1}{2}$ teaspoons salt
1.5kg (3lb) chicken pieces
2 tablespoons vegetable oil
2 medium onions, peeled, halved and sliced
   paper-thin
1 tablespoon paprika
freshly ground black pepper
350ml (12fl oz) chicken stock
150ml ($\frac{1}{4}$ pint) soured cream
parsley sprigs, to garnish

Preparation time: 15 minutes
Cooking time: 1$\frac{1}{4}$ hours
Oven: 180°C, 350°F, Gas Mark 4

1. Mix the flour with $\frac{1}{2}$ teaspoon of the salt in a polythene bag and toss the chicken pieces in it. Tip the remaining flour into a saucer and set aside.
2. Heat the oil in a large heavy frying pan and slowly brown the chicken on all sides. Remove and drain on paper towels. Place in a casserole.
3. Stir the reserved flour into the oil and cook, stirring, on low heat for 1 minute. Add the onions, paprika, remaining salt, pepper and stock. Bring to the boil, stirring.
4. Pour the sauce over the chicken, cover and cook in a preheated oven for 1 hour.
5. Place the chicken on a serving dish and skim off or blot up any excess fat from the gravy. Stir the soured cream into the gravy and pour over the chicken. Serve immediately garnished with parsley sprigs, if liked.

Serves 6

Nutrition content per serving   Carbohydrate: 9g   Fat: 25g
Fibre: 1g   Kilocalories: 405

Chicken Paprikash.

CHICKEN CACCIATORE

This is a traditional Italian recipe in which the chicken is flavoured with garlic, tomatoes and basil.

2kg (4lb) chicken, or 4 large chicken portions
3 tablespoons oil
2 large onions, peeled and sliced
2 garlic cloves, peeled and crushed
1 × 425g (15oz) can tomatoes
2 tablespoons chopped fresh parsley, or
  1 tablespoon dried parsley
1 teaspoon dried basil
1 tablespoon tomato purée (optional)
150ml ($\frac{1}{4}$ pint) red wine
salt
freshly ground black pepper

Preparation time: 15 minutes
Cooking time: about 1 hour
Oven: 160°C, 325°F, Gas Mark 3

1. Cut the chicken into 8 pieces (or halve the portions) and remove the skin.
2. Heat the oil in a pan and fry the chicken pieces until browned all over. Transfer to a casserole.
3. Add the onions and garlic to the pan and fry until golden brown. Add the tomatoes with their juice, the parsley, basil, tomato purée (if using) and wine, then bring to the boil. Add plenty of salt and pepper.
4. Pour over the chicken, cover the casserole and cook in a preheated oven for about 1 hour or until tender.
5. Adjust the seasoning and serve very hot with pasta.

Serves 4

Nutrition content per serving Carbohydrate: 5g Fat: 21g
Fibre: 2g Kilocalories: 520

SOMERSET CHICKEN

1 tablespoon corn oil
100g (4oz) butter
1 chicken, about 1.5kg (3lb), cut into portions
1 small onion, peeled and sliced
25g (1oz) plain flour
450ml ($\frac{3}{4}$ pint) dry cider
120ml (4fl oz) chicken stock
1 teaspoon dried mixed herbs
salt
freshly ground black pepper
1kg (2lb) cooking apples, peeled, cored and
  thickly sliced

Preparation time: 30 minutes
Cooking time: $1\frac{1}{2}$–$1\frac{3}{4}$ hours
Oven: 180°C, 350°F, Gas Mark 4

1. Heat the oil and half the butter in a frying pan, add the chicken and fry on both sides until golden brown. Remove to a casserole.
2. Add the onion to the pan and fry until tender. Sprinkle in the flour and cook, stirring constantly, until light brown. Gradually stir in the cider, stock and herbs and bring to the boil, stirring constantly. Cook until thickened. Season to taste and pour over the chicken.
3. Cover the casserole and cook in a preheated oven for 30 minutes.
4. Meanwhile, melt the remaining butter in a pan, add the apples and cook for 2 minutes, stirring occasionally. Spoon the apples on top of the chicken, cover the casserole again and cook for a further 30–45 minutes or until the chicken is very tender.

Serves 6

Nutrition content per serving Carbohydrate: 17g Fat: 22g
Fibre: 3g Kilocalories: 354

LEFT: Chicken Cacciatore. ABOVE: Somerset Chicken.

GUINEA FOWL WITH GRAPES

*2 young oven-ready guinea fowl, about 450g (1lb)
  each, with giblets*
1 small onion
½ teaspoon dried thyme
salt
freshly ground black pepper
4 streaky bacon rashers, rind removed
350g (12oz) black grapes
2 tablespoons plain flour
TO SERVE:
*2 slices of bread, crusts removed, quartered
  diagonally*
oil for frying
75g (3oz) black grapes, halved and seeded

Preparation time: 45–60 minutes
Cooking time: 1¾–2 hours
Oven: 160°C, 325°F, Gas Mark 3

1. Remove the giblets from the birds and put them into a saucepan with the onion, thyme and water to cover. Add salt and pepper. Bring to the boil and simmer for 30 minutes. Strain and reserve 150ml (¼ pint) of the stock.
2. Cover each guinea fowl with 2 rashers of bacon (if the birds are already larded remove the plain fat). Put the birds into a deep casserole, side by side.
3. Pack the grapes all round the birds. Cover with a tight-fitting lid or foil.
4. Cook in a preheated oven for 1¾–2 hours or until the birds feel well cooked and tender when pierced through the breast with a pointed knife.
5. Lift out the guinea fowl and keep hot. Rub the grapes and liquid through a strainer into a saucepan.
6. Blend the flour with the reserved giblet stock, stir into the grape purée and bring to the boil, stirring until thickened. Add salt and pepper to taste.
7. Fry the bread triangles in oil until golden brown.
8. Remove the bacon from the guinea fowl, cut the birds in half and serve with some sauce poured over them. Garnish with the bread croûtons and halved grapes. Serve the remaining sauce separately.

Serves 4

Nutrition content per serving   Carbohydrate: 30g   Fat: 24g
Fibre: 1g   Kilocalories: 487

COQ AU VIN BLANC

25g (1oz) butter
1 tablespoon oil
*1 × 2.5cm (1 inch) thick streaky bacon rasher,
  rind removed, chopped*
100g (4oz) button onions, peeled
1 garlic clove, peeled and crushed
½ small chicken
200ml (⅓ pint) dry white wine
150ml (¼ pint) chicken stock
1 bouquet garni
a large pinch of dried mixed herbs
salt
freshly ground black pepper
50g (2oz) button mushrooms
15g (½ oz) plain flour

Preparation time: 20 minutes
Cooking time: 1¼–1½ hours
Oven: 160°C, 325°F, Gas Mark 3

1. Melt 15g (½oz) of the butter with the oil in a frying pan. Add the bacon and fry until golden brown. Transfer the bacon to a flameproof casserole. Fry the onions and garlic in the pan until lightly browned and add to the casserole. Cut the chicken in half or into four pieces and put in the pan. Brown on all sides, then add to the casserole.
2. Remove excess fat from the frying pan. Stir in the wine and stock and bring to the boil. Pour into the casserole and add the bouquet garni, herbs and salt and pepper to taste. Cover tightly. Cook in a preheated oven for about 1 hour.
3. Add the mushrooms and continue cooking for 15 minutes.
4. Discard the bouquet garni. Cream the remaining butter and the flour together to make a paste and whisk this gradually into the casserole. Bring to the boil on top of the stove. Adjust the seasoning and serve with parsleyed new potatoes.

Serves 2

Nutrition content per serving   Carbohydrate: 9g   Fat: 32g
Fibre: 2g   Kilocalories: 540

TOP: Guinea Fowl with Grapes.
BOTTOM: Coq au Vin Blanc.

GOLDEN CHICKEN CASSEROLE

Turmeric has very little flavour but gives a glowing golden colour to this casserole. Yellow food colouring will do as a substitute. Yellow peppers can be found in many of the bigger supermarkets and greengrocers. If they are not available, use a red pepper.

4 chicken quarters
4 tablespoons plain flour
salt
freshly ground black pepper
4 tablespoons vegetable oil
25g (1oz) butter
1 large onion, peeled, quartered and sliced
1 teaspoon turmeric
1 × 400g (14oz) can tomatoes
300ml ($\frac{1}{2}$ pint) medium cider
100g (4oz) sweetcorn kernels
1 yellow pepper, seeded and cut in rings
1 Golden Delicious apple, cored and sliced

Preparation time: 30 minutes
Cooking time: $1\frac{1}{4}$ hours
Oven: 180°C, 350°F, Gas Mark 4

1. Toss the chicken quarters in flour seasoned with salt and pepper to coat them thoroughly. Heat the oil in a frying pan, add the chicken and brown lightly on all sides. Remove to a 2.25 litre (4 pint) casserole.
2. Add the butter to the frying pan, then the onion and fry until lightly golden. Stir in any remaining seasoned flour with the turmeric and cook for 1 minute.
3. Drain the liquid from the tomatoes. Add the liquid to the frying pan with the cider. Cook until thickened, stirring constantly.
4. Cut the tomatoes into quarters. Add to the casserole with the sweetcorn and pepper rings. Pour over the cider sauce. Cover the casserole and cook in a preheated oven for about 40 minutes.
5. Stir in the apple and cook for a further 15 minutes. Taste and adjust the seasoning.

Serves 4

Nutrition content per serving   Carbohydrate: 25g   Fat: 32g
Fibre: 4g   Kilocalories: 606

CHICKEN IN SWEET & SOUR SAUCE

8 chicken drumsticks
salt
freshly ground black pepper
2 teaspoons ground ginger
25g (1oz) butter
2 tablespoons cornflour
5 tablespoons vinegar
2 teaspoons soy sauce
3–4 tablespoons brown sugar
300ml ($\frac{1}{2}$ pint) chicken stock
1 × 400g (14oz) can pineapple pieces
4 tomatoes, skinned and quartered
1 red pepper, seeded and sliced

Preparation time: 25 minutes
Cooking time: 1 hour
Oven: 180°C, 350°F, Gas Mark 4

1. Season chicken with salt and pepper. Rub ginger into the surface of each joint and dot each with a knob of butter. Grill until golden and transfer to a casserole dish.
2. In a pan blend the cornflour with a little cold water. Stir in the vinegar, soy sauce, sugar and chicken stock. Bring slowly to the boil, stirring until thickened. Stir in the contents of the can of pineapple, the tomatoes and red pepper.
3. Pour the sauce over the chicken joints. Cover and cook in a preheated oven for about 30 minutes.

Serves 4

Nutrition content per serving   Carbohydrate: 44g   Fat: 12g
Fibre: 2g   Kilocalories: 392

TOP: Golden Chicken Casserole; BOTTOM: Chicken in Sweet & Sour Sauce.

CHICKEN & MUSHROOM PIE

1.5kg (3lb) oven-ready chicken with giblets
1 bouquet garni
1 small onion, peeled and quartered
salt
6–8 peppercorns
25g (1oz) butter
2 leeks, trimmed and thinly sliced
100g (4oz) button mushrooms, sliced
1 teaspoon plain flour
100g (4oz) low-fat soft cheese
2 tablespoons chopped fresh parsley
TOPPING:
450g (1lb) potatoes, peeled
225g (8oz) carrots, sliced
25g (1oz) butter
1 egg
pinch of grated nutmeg
freshly ground black pepper

Preparation time: 25 minutes
Cooking time: $1\frac{3}{4}$ hours
Oven: 190°C, 375°F, Gas Mark 5

1. Wash the chicken and giblets and put them in a large saucepan with the bouquet garni, onion, salt and peppercorns. Cover with water, bring to the boil and skim. Cover the pan and simmer for about 1 hour, or until the chicken is cooked.
2. Lift out the chicken and, when it is cool enough to handle, skin it and cut the meat from the bones. Slice the liver. Place the chicken pieces in a baking dish and set aside. Reserve the chicken stock for soups.
3. Melt the butter in a small pan and fry the leeks and mushrooms over a moderate heat for 3 minutes, stirring once or twice. Stir in the flour, then the cheese and parsley. Simmer for 3 minutes, then spread over the chicken.
4. Cook the potatoes and carrots in boiling salted water for 15–20 minutes, or until they are tender. Drain and mash them and beat in the butter and egg. Season the mixture with nutmeg, salt and pepper.
5. Spread the vegetable topping evenly over the chicken, then fork it up into peaks.
6. Bake in a preheated oven for 20–25 minutes until the topping is well browned.

Serves 6

Nutrition content per serving   Carbohydrate: 19g   Fat: 16g
Fibre: 4g   Kilocalories: 383

CHICKEN WITH LEMON & WALNUTS

4 chicken portions
salt
freshly ground black pepper
40g (1½ oz) butter
2 tablespoons chopped spring onions
1 tablespoon plain flour
1 teaspoon ground ginger
450ml (¾ pint) beef stock
1 tablespoon black treacle
grated rind of 1 lemon
2 tablespoons lemon juice
50g (2oz) walnut pieces
TO GARNISH (OPTIONAL):
julienne strips of lemon rind
walnut halves
parsley sprigs

Preparation time: 20 minutes
Cooking time: 1 hour
Oven: 180°C, 350°F, Gas Mark 4

1. Sprinkle the chicken with salt and pepper. Melt the butter in a pan and fry the chicken until browned all over. Transfer to a casserole.
2. Fry the onions in the same fat until soft. Stir in the flour and ginger and cook for 1 minute. Gradually add the stock and bring to the boil. Simmer for 1 minute.
3. Stir in the black treacle, lemon rind and juice and walnuts. Pour over the chicken and cover the casserole.
4. Cook in a preheated oven for 1 hour. Spoon off any excess fat from the surface and adjust the seasoning.
5. Garnish with lemon rind, walnuts and parsley, if liked.

Serves 4

Nutrition content per serving   Carbohydrate: 7g   Fat: 22g
Fibre: 1g   Kilocalories: 374

TOP: Chicken & Mushroom Pie; BOTTOM: Chicken with Lemon & Walnuts.

CASSEROLE OF PHEASANT WITH DRIED APRICOTS

25g (1oz) butter
2 oven-ready pheasants
225g (8oz) small onions or shallots, peeled
1 tablespoon plain flour
450ml ($\frac{3}{4}$ pint) chicken stock
1 tablespoon clear honey
2 teaspoons grated orange rind
3 tablespoons orange juice
1 bay leaf
225g (8oz) dried whole apricots, soaked for 2–3
*   hours and drained*
salt
freshly ground black pepper

Preparation time: 30 minutes, plus soaking
Cooking time: 2 hours
Oven: 180°C, 350°F, Gas Mark 4

1. Melt the butter in a flameproof casserole and fry the pheasants over moderate heat for 10 minutes, turning the birds frequently to brown them evenly. Lift out the pheasants and keep them warm. Fry the onions in the casserole for 2–3 minutes, stirring them once or twice, then stir in the flour. Pour on the chicken stock, stirring all the time, then add the honey, orange rind, orange juice, bay leaf and apricots, and season with salt and pepper. Bring the sauce to the boil, stirring occasionally.
2. Return the pheasants to the casserole and cover. Cook in a preheated oven for 1½ hours, or until the birds are tender.
3. Lift out the pheasants and cut them into joints – a pair of poultry shears is a help. Lift out the onions and apricots with a draining spoon and arrange them around the pheasant. Discard the bay leaf.
4. Boil the sauce over moderate heat for 5–10 minutes to reduce and thicken it. Taste it and adjust the seasoning if necessary. Pour the sauce over the pheasants.

Serves 6

Nutrition content per serving   Carbohydrate: 23g   Fat: 10g
Fibre: 10g   Kilocalories: 267

LEFT: Turkey Beanpot.
ABOVE: Casserole of Pheasant with Dried Apricots.

TURKEY BEANPOT

25g (1oz) butter
1 tablespoon vegetable oil
750g (1½ lb) turkey thigh meat, skinned and cut
*   into 2.5cm (1 inch) cubes*
1 large onion, peeled and sliced
1 garlic clove, peeled and crushed
1 red pepper, seeded and chopped
1 tablespoon plain flour
150ml ($\frac{1}{4}$ pint) red wine
1 × 425g (15oz) can tomatoes
150ml ($\frac{1}{4}$ pint) chicken stock
salt
freshly ground black pepper
1 teaspoon ground ginger
1 tablespoon soy sauce
1 tablespoon Worcestershire sauce
1 × 200g (7oz) can butter beans, drained
1 × 425g (15oz) can red kidney beans, drained

Preparation time: 15 minutes
Cooking time: about 1 hour
Oven: 180°C, 350°F, Gas Mark 4

1. Heat the butter and oil in a pan and fry the turkey until lightly browned. Transfer to a casserole.
2. Fry the onion and garlic in the same fat until soft. Add the pepper and continue cooking for 2 minutes.
3. Stir in the flour and cook for 1 minute, then add the wine, tomatoes and stock and bring to the boil. Pour into the casserole.
4. Add the remaining ingredients. Cover and cook in a preheated oven for 1 hour.

Serves 4

Nutrition content per serving   Carbohydrate: 29g   Fat: 16g
Fibre: 11g   Kilocalories: 478

RAGGED RABBIT

25g (1oz) butter
1 tablespoon vegetable oil
450g (1lb) boneless rabbit, diced
4 bacon rashers, rind removed, chopped
350g (12oz) pickling onions, peeled
2 tablespoons plain flour
150ml (¼ pint) dry white wine
450ml (¾ pint) chicken stock
4 carrots, peeled and diced
8–12 prunes, soaked (if necessary)
salt
freshly ground black pepper
1 bay leaf
4 tablespoons double cream (optional)

Preparation time: 25 minutes
Cooking time: 1½ hours
Oven: 180°C, 350°F, Gas Mark 4

1. Heat the butter with the oil in a pan and fry the rabbit until browned. Transfer to a casserole.
2. Fry the bacon and onions in the same fat until lightly coloured. Sprinkle in the flour and cook for 1 minute.
3. Gradually add the wine and stock, bring to the boil and simmer for 2 minutes.
4. Add the carrots, prunes, plenty of salt and pepper and the bay leaf, then pour over the rabbit. Mix well and cover the casserole tightly.
5. Cook in a preheated oven for 1½ hours or until tender.
6. Taste and adjust the seasoning, discard the bay leaf and stir in the cream (if using).

Serves 4

Nutrition content per serving   Carbohydrate: 35g   Fat: 31g
Fibre: 11g   Kilocalories: 535

RABBIT & ONION CASSEROLE

2 medium onions, peeled and sliced
3 tablespoons vegetable oil
8 small rabbit joints
seasoned flour
1 tablespoon French mustard
1 tablespoon demerara sugar
600ml (1 pint) chicken stock
1 bay leaf
4 slices French bread
50g (2oz) Cheddar cheese, grated
1 tablespoon chopped fresh parsley

Preparation time: 20 minutes
Cooking time: about 1 hour
Oven: 190°C, 375°F, Gas Mark 5

1. Fry the onions in the oil for 2–3 minutes. Dust the rabbit joints in the seasoned flour. Add the rabbit joints to the pan and fry until lightly browned on all sides. Add the French mustard, demerara sugar, chicken stock and bay leaf, and bring to the boil.
2. Transfer to a casserole, cover and cook in a preheated oven for 40 minutes.
3. Uncover the casserole, top the rabbit and onion with the slices of French bread and sprinkle with grated cheese. Return the uncovered casserole to the oven to cook for a further 5 minutes. Sprinkle with chopped fresh parsley and serve with a green vegetable and boiled potatoes.

Serves 4

Nutrition content per serving   Carbohydrate: 25g   Fat: 21g
Fibre: 2g   Kilocalories: 403

TOP: Rabbit & Onion Casserole; BOTTOM: Ragged Rabbit.

VENISON IN BLACKCURRANT SAUCE

750g (1½ lb) boneless venison, cut into 2.5cm
 (1 inch) cubes
1 large onion, peeled and sliced
1 carrot, peeled and sliced
12 black peppercorns
2 bay leaves
450ml (¾ pint) red wine
50g (2oz) dripping or vegetable fat
1 tablespoon plain flour
300ml (½ pint) beef stock
350g (12oz) blackcurrants
pinch of sugar
triangular croûtons, to garnish

Preparation time: 20 minutes, plus
marinating overnight
Cooking time: 2–3 hours
Oven: 160°C, 325°F, Gas Mark 3

1. Place the venison in a deep dish with the
onion, carrot, peppercorns, bay leaves and
wine. Cover and leave to marinate overnight in
the refrigerator.
2. Drain the meat and vegetables separately.
Reserve the red wine and bay leaves but
discard the peppercorns.
3. Melt the dripping in a flameproof casserole,
add the meat and brown. Remove from the pan
with a slotted spoon.
4. Add the drained carrot and onion to the pan
and cook for a few minutes. Add the flour and
cook for 1–2 minutes, then add the stock, red
wine, bay leaves, blackcurrants, salt and
pepper. Return the venison to the casserole.
5. Cover and cook in a preheated oven for 2–3
hours, depending on the age of the venison,
until the meat is tender.
6. Remove the meat carefully from the sauce
and place on a heated serving dish. Purée the
sauce in a food processor or blender. Do not
over-purée or the pips in the blackcurrants will
become gritty. Strain the sauce into a clean
pan. Reheat and, if necessary, boil to reduce
until thick enough to coat the back of a spoon.
Adjust the seasoning, adding the sugar.
7. Pour the sauce over the meat and garnish
with the fried croûtons.

Serves 4

Nutrition content per serving   Carbohydrate: 13g   Fat: 19g
Fibre: 9g   Kilocalories: 383

TOP: Venison in Blackcurrant Sauce; BOTTOM:
Pigeons with Black Cherries.

PIGEONS WITH BLACK CHERRIES

4 oven-ready pigeons
salt
freshly ground black pepper
2 tablespoons vegetable oil
175g (6oz) pickling onions, peeled
2 tablespoons plain flour
1 × 425g (15oz) can black cherries
about 150ml (¼ pint) beef stock
2 tablespoons wine vinegar
2 tablespoons brandy
1–2 fresh thyme sprigs
FLEURONS:
100g (4oz) puff pastry
milk or beaten egg, to glaze

Preparation time: 15 minutes
Cooking time: about 1½ hours
Oven: 160°C, 325°F, Gas Mark 3; then 200°C,
400°F, Gas Mark 6

1. Halve the pigeons and remove the backbone,
using a pair of poultry shears, kitchen scissors
or a sharp knife. Sprinkle the birds with salt
and pepper.
2. Heat the oil in a pan and fry the pieces until
browned. Transfer to a casserole.
3. Fry the onions in the same fat until lightly
browned. Stir in the flour and cook for 1
minute.
4. Drain juices from the cherries and make up
to 450ml (¾ pint) with stock. Gradually add to
the pan and bring to the boil. Add the cherries
with plenty of salt and pepper.
5. Add the wine vinegar, brandy and thyme
and pour over the pigeons. Cover the casserole.
6. Cook in a preheated oven for about 1½ hours
or until the pigeons are very tender.
7. To make the pastry fleurons, roll out the
puff pastry and cut into 6cm (2½ inch) crescents,
using a fluted pastry cutter. Arrange on a
baking sheet, brush with milk or beaten egg
and bake in a preheated oven at the higher
temperature for 10–15 minutes until golden
brown. Cool on a wire rack.
8. Discard the sprigs of thyme and serve the
casserole garnished with pastry fleurons.

Variation: Use 4 partridges instead of the
pigeons and leave them whole.

Serves 4

Nutrition content per serving   Carbohydrate: 38g   Fat: 26g
Fibre: 2g   Kilocalories: 484

Seafood
◆
CASSEROLES

*Casseroles that include fish and shellfish
are very popular family supper dishes,
perhaps because the fish is easy to eat (no bones!)
and it is in a well-flavoured sauce.
The recipes in this chapter will certainly
tempt any would-be fish hater.
Here you'll find cod steaks baked on a layer of
buttered spinach and topped with a
cheese sauce, halibut cooked in a thick
tomato-wine sauce, a casserole of white fish,
prawns, crab and mussels sauced with lobster bisque,
white fish fillets with mushrooms and peas
in a mustard cream sauce,
a layered gratin of prawns,
hard-boiled egg and tomatoes
topped with a rich cheese sauce, smoked
haddock and mixed vegetables in a creamy
custard, and a Scandinavian dish
of anchovies and potatoes.*

Bouillabaisse Casserole (see recipe on page 68).

BOUILLABAISSE CASSEROLE

A true bouillabaisse is made using at least 8 types of fish and shellfish but many of the authentic types are only available in Mediterranean areas. Your fishmonger should be able to help with a good selection.

1.25kg (2½ lb) mixed fish and shellfish
6 tablespoons oil
2 large onions, peeled and thinly sliced
2 celery sticks, thinly sliced
2 carrots, peeled and diced
2 garlic cloves, peeled and crushed
450g (1lb) tomatoes, peeled and sliced
1 bouquet garni
salt
freshly ground black pepper
grated rind of ½ lemon
juice of 1 lemon
pinch of saffron or turmeric
about 300ml (½ pint) white wine
TO GARNISH:
fresh dill or other herb sprigs
few whole prawns or crayfish (optional)

Preparation time: 20 minutes
Cooking time: about 50 minutes
Oven: 180°C, 350°F, Gas Mark 4

1. Clean the fish, remove all the skin and any loose bones, wash and cut into pieces about 5cm (2 inches). Remove the shellfish from the shells except for prawns or crayfish for garnish and wash thoroughly.
2. Heat the oil in a pan and fry the onions, celery, carrots and garlic gently, until soft but only lightly coloured.
3. Add the tomatoes, bouquet garni, salt, pepper, lemon rind, juice and saffron or turmeric and turn into a casserole.
4. Lay the fish over the vegetables, then add enough wine almost to cover the fish.
5. Cover the casserole and cook in a preheated oven for about 50 minutes, until the fish is tender. Discard the bouquet garni and taste and adjust the seasoning.
6. Serve very hot, garnished with herb sprigs and a few whole prawns or crayfish.
Accompany with crusty bread or boiled rice.

Serves 4

Nutrition content per serving   Carbohydrate: 10g   Fat: 23g
Fibre: 4g   Kilocalories: 534

MIXED FISH CASSEROLE WITH MUSTARD CREAM

50g (2oz) butter
3 medium onions, peeled and finely chopped
2 garlic cloves, peeled and crushed
1 bouquet garni
2 cloves
150ml (¼ pint) dry white wine
150ml (¼ pint) fish stock or very light chicken stock
juice of ½ lemon
salt
freshly ground black pepper
750g (1¾lb) mixed white fish fillets (plaice, cod, haddock, lemon sole, huss, whiting), skinned and cut into 5cm (2 inch) pieces
100g (4oz) button mushrooms, sliced
100g (4oz) fresh or frozen peas
1 teaspoon Dijon mustard
4 tablespoons double cream
TO GARNISH:
puff pastry fleurons (see page 65)
watercress sprigs

Preparation time: 20 minutes
Cooking time: 35 minutes
Oven: 160°C, 325°F, Gas Mark 3

1. Melt the butter in a frying pan, add the onions and fry gently until softened.
2. Stir in the garlic, bouquet garni, cloves, white wine and stock. Bring to the boil and simmer for 5 minutes. Allow to cool slightly, then pour into a casserole. Stir in the lemon juice and salt and pepper to taste and add the fish pieces.
3. Cover and cook in a preheated oven for 25 minutes.
4. Add the mushrooms and peas and continue cooking for 10 minutes. Discard the bouquet garni.
5. Stir the mustard into the cream and stir into the casserole carefully – do not break the fish. Adjust the seasoning.
6. Garnish with pastry fleurons and watercress, and serve with sauté potatoes and mange tout peas.

Serves 4

Nutrition content per serving   Carbohydrate: 15g   Fat: 27g
Fibre: 4g   Kilocalories: 444

Mixed Fish Casserole with Mustard Cream.

HALIBUT CATALAN

Around the Mediterranean they love to cook
white fish in thick sauces, highly flavoured with
tomatoes, onion and garlic. Halibut lends itself
well to this particular combination of flavours.

6 tablespoons olive oil
juice of 1 lemon
salt
freshly ground black pepper
4 slices filleted halibut or halibut steaks
1 small onion, peeled and finely chopped
1 garlic clove, peeled and crushed
1 tablespoon plain flour
225g (8oz) tomatoes, skinned, seeded and chopped
1 tablespoon tomato purée
300ml (½ pint) dry white wine
TO FINISH (OPTIONAL):
50g (2oz) finely chopped hazelnuts
2 tablespoons chopped fresh parsley

Preparation time: 30 minutes, plus
marinating
Cooking time: 40 minutes
Oven: 180°C, 350°F, Gas Mark 4

1. Mix together 4 tablespoons of the oil, the
lemon juice, and salt and pepper to taste.
Leave the halibut to soak in this marinade for
1–2 hours, basting and turning occasionally.
2. Heat the remaining oil in a deep flameproof
casserole. Add the onion and garlic and fry
gently until golden. Stir in the flour, tomatoes,
tomato purée and white wine. Slowly bring to
the boil, stirring constantly.
3. Add the marinated halibut, coating the fish
with the sauce, and cover with a lid or foil.
Transfer to a preheated oven and bake for
about 20 minutes or until the fish is tender and
will flake easily with a fork.
4. Remove from the oven and top with the
chopped hazelnuts and parsley, if using. Serve
immediately.

Serves 4

Nutrition content per serving   Carbohydrate: 7g   Fat: 31g
Fibre: 2g   Kilocalories: 440

COD BAKE

750g (1½ lb) fresh spinach, or 1 × 290g (10oz)
* packet frozen chopped spinach*
salt
freshly ground black pepper
¼ teaspoon grated nutmeg
50g (2oz) butter
4 cod steaks
CHEESE SAUCE:
25g (1oz) butter
25g (1oz) plain flour
450ml (¾ pint) hot milk
100g (4oz) Cheddar cheese, grated

Preparation time: 20 minutes
Cooking time: 40–50 minutes
Oven: 190°C, 375°F, Gas Mark 5

1. Wash the fresh spinach and place in a large
saucepan with salt to taste. Heat gently until
juices flow from the spinach, then cover the
pan with a lid and cook gently for 5–10
minutes or until the spinach is tender. Drain
well and chop finely or purée in a blender. If
using frozen spinach, cook according to packet
directions.
2. Season the cooked spinach with plenty of
black pepper and the nutmeg and stir in half of
the butter. Place in the bottom of a shallow
ovenproof dish.
3. Fry the cod steaks in the remaining butter
for 2–3 minutes on each side, then place on top
of the spinach in the dish.
4. To prepare the cheese sauce, melt the butter
in a pan. Stir in the flour and cook for 2–3
minutes, stirring constantly. Remove the pan
from the heat and add the milk gradually,
stirring vigorously. When all the milk has been
incorporated, return the pan to the heat. Bring
slowly to the boil, stirring constantly. Lower
the heat, add 50g (2oz) of the grated cheese and
cook for 2–3 minutes or until cheese melts in
the sauce, stirring constantly.
5. Cover the fish with the cheese sauce and
sprinkle with the remaining grated cheese.
Bake in a preheated oven for 20–30 minutes or
until the fish is cooked and the top of the
casserole is lightly browned and bubbling. Test
the fish with a fork: the flesh should flake
easily. Serve immediately.

Serves 4

Nutrition content per serving   Carbohydrate: 13g   Fat: 26g
Fibre: 4g   Kilocalories: 418

TOP: Cod Bake; BOTTOM: Halibut Catalan.

PRAWN GRATIN

225g (8oz) peeled prawns
2 hard-boiled eggs, chopped
4 tomatoes, skinned and sliced
25g (1oz) Gruyère or Emmental cheese, grated
CHEESE SAUCE:
25g (1oz) butter
25g (1oz) plain flour
300ml (½ pint) milk
25–50g (1–2oz) Gruyère cheese, grated
1 teaspoon paprika
1 tablespoon cream (optional)
salt
freshly ground black pepper

Preparation time: 30 minutes
Cooking time: 25 minutes
Oven: 190°C, 375°F, Gas Mark 5

1. Butter an ovenproof dish and arrange in it the prawns, eggs and tomatoes, in layers.
2. To make the cheese sauce, melt the butter gently, then remove from the heat and stir in the flour. Gradually stir in the milk, then return to the heat and bring to the boil, stirring constantly. Simmer for 3–4 minutes, stirring frequently. Stir the cheese and paprika into the sauce. Add the cream, if using, and salt and pepper to taste, then pour over the dish.
3. Sprinkle with the cheese and bake in a preheated oven for 15 minutes.

Serves 4

Nutrition content per serving   Carbohydrate: 4g   Fat: 19g
Fibre: 0g   Kilocalories: 276

JANSSON'S TEMPTATION

12 anchovy fillets, or 1 × 50g (2oz) can
450g (1lb) potatoes, peeled and cut into chips
2 large onions, peeled and finely sliced
1 garlic clove, peeled and crushed
1 tablespoon chopped fresh parsley
freshly ground black pepper
300ml (½ pint) single cream
40g (1½ oz) butter

Preparation time: 40 minutes
Cooking time: about 1 hour
Oven: 220°C, 425°F, Gas Mark 7

1. If using canned anchovies, drain and reserve a little of the liquid. Cut each fillet into four.

2. Well butter an ovenproof dish, then layer in it the potatoes, onions, garlic, anchovies and parsley, seasoning with black pepper and finishing with a layer of potatoes. Drizzle on a little of the anchovy liquid, if available. Pour over half the cream and dot with the butter.
3. Bake in a preheated oven until the potatoes are lightly coloured, then pour over the remaining cream and cook until tender.

Serves 4

Nutrition content per serving   Carbohydrate: 26g   Fat: 26g
Fibre: 3g   Kilocalories: 366

SMOKED HADDOCK SPECIAL

1kg (2lb) smoked haddock fillets, skinned and
  halved
2 teaspoons lemon juice
salt
freshly ground black pepper
25g (1oz) butter
1 medium onion, peeled and finely chopped
150ml (¼ pint) milk
1 bay leaf
1 tablespoon cornflour
150ml (¼ pint) single cream
1 × 225g (8oz) packet frozen mixed vegetables
  (including sweetcorn), thawed
2 tablespoons chopped fresh parsley
50g (2oz) Cheddar cheese, grated

Preparation time: 30 minutes
Cooking time: 40 minutes
Oven: 160°C, 325°F, Gas Mark 3

1. Place the fish in a flameproof casserole, pour over the lemon juice and season.
2. Melt the butter in a small frying pan, add the onion and fry until softened. Pour over the fish and add the milk and bay leaf. Cover and cook in a preheated oven for 20 minutes.
3. Remove the bay leaf. Dissolve the cornflour in the cream and pour into the casserole. Bring to the boil on top of the stove, stirring gently.
4. Add the vegetables and parsley and mix carefully. Sprinkle the cheese over the top.
5. Return to the oven and bake for 20 minutes.

Serves 4

Nutrition content per serving   Carbohydrate: 13g   Fat: 20g
Fibre: 3g   Kilocalories: 409

CLOCKWISE FROM THE TOP: Prawn Gratin; Jansson's Temptation; Smoked Haddock Special.

LAYERED FISH PIE

450g (1lb) firm white fish fillets, e.g. cod or
    haddock
1 bay leaf
6 white peppercorns
1.2 litres (2 pints) milk
2 tablespoons olive oil
2 large onions, peeled and finely sliced
450g (1lb) potatoes, finely sliced
2 garlic cloves, peeled
grated nutmeg
salt
freshly ground black pepper
6 eggs (size 1 or 2)
450g (1lb) tomatoes, finely sliced
½ teaspoon dried dill
50g (2oz) Cheddar or Lancashire cheese, grated

Preparation time: 20–25 minutes
Cooking time: about 40 minutes
Oven: 180°C, 350°F, Gas Mark 4

1. Put the fish into a shallow pan with the bay
leaf, peppercorns and half the milk. Bring to
the boil and simmer gently, covered, for 15
minutes or until the fish flakes easily.
2. In another pan, heat the oil, add the onions
and fry gently for 15 minutes until golden.
3. Put the potatoes in layers in a saucepan,
sprinkling each layer with a few slivers from
one of the garlic cloves, nutmeg, salt and
pepper. Cover with the remaining milk, bring
to the boil, then simmer gently for about 8–10
minutes until they are just done.
4. Hard-boil 4 of the eggs. Cool.
5. Rub a casserole with the remaining garlic
clove and spoon the onions into the bottom to
make a layer. Remove the fish from its milk
with a slotted spoon and arrange on top of the
onions. Strain the milk and reserve.
6. Add the tomatoes to the oil left in the onion
pan and stir-fry over a high heat for 2–3
minutes until beginning to soften.
7. Arrange the tomatoes on top of the fish and
sprinkle with the dill. Bury the garlic clove
used to rub the casserole into the mixture.
8. Drain the potatoes, reserving the milk. Shell
the eggs and slice. Arrange a layer of egg slices
over the tomatoes, then cover with the
potatoes.
9. Beat the remaining 2 eggs well, then whisk
into all the reserved milk. Pour over the dish,

TOP: Layered Fish Pie; BOTTOM: Seafood Casserole.

adding a little extra milk if necessary, so that
the liquid is level with the potatoes. Sprinkle
the cheese on top.
10. Cook in a preheated oven for 12–20
minutes until the 'custard' is very lightly set –
not too solid or the pie will be dry.

Serves 4

Nutrition content per serving   Carbohydrate: 42g   Fat: 34g
Fibre: 5g   Kilocalories: 650

SEAFOOD CASSEROLE

450g (1lb) firm white fish fillets, skinned
150ml (¼ pint) dry white wine
1 small onion, peeled and chopped
2 bay leaves
parsley sprig
2 teaspoons cornflour
1 × 400g (14oz) can lobster bisque
juice of ½ lemon
salt
freshly ground black pepper
225g (8oz) peeled prawns
100g (4oz) crab meat, frozen and thawed or
    canned
100g (4oz) jar of mussels (optional)
3 tablespoons fresh white breadcrumbs
15g (½ oz) butter

Preparation time: 15 minutes
Cooking time: 45 minutes
Oven: 220°C, 425°F, Gas Mark 7

1. Cut the white fish into large chunks and
place in a saucepan. Add the wine, onion, bay
leaves and parsley and bring to the boil, then
simmer gently for 5 minutes.
2. Lift out the fish and reserve it. Strain the
fish liquor, blend the cornflour into it and
return to the saucepan. Add the lobster bisque
and bring to the boil, stirring constantly, then
cook gently for 2 minutes. Add the lemon juice
and season to taste.
3. Place the prawns, crab, mussels and
reserved white fish in an ovenproof dish and
pour the sauce over. Sprinkle the top with
breadcrumbs and dot with butter.
4. Cook in a preheated oven for 30 minutes or
until lightly browned and heated through.

Serves 6

Nutrition content per serving   Carbohydrate: 8g   Fat: 7g
Fibre: 0g   Kilocalories: 211

Vegetable
♦
CASSEROLES

Vegetable casseroles are extremely convenient because they can usually be prepared ahead of time, and put in to cook with the main dish they are to accompany. And there are some vegetable casseroles that are substantial enough to be main dishes on their own.

In this chapter, there are many ideas for accompanying vegetable casseroles, such as red cabbage with apples and raisins, celery, carrot and parsnip with fresh coriander, courgettes in a rich cheese custard, tomatoes baked in cream with basil and parsley, and aubergines layered with tomatoes and yogurt.

For a change from a meat main dish, you might like to try a casserole of aduki beans, carrots, onion and cabbage topped with sliced potatoes, or savoury crumble of carrots and sweetcorn.

TOP: Red Cabbage Casserole (see recipe on page 79);
BOTTOM: Casserole of Chestnuts, Apple & Prunes (see recipe on page 80).

TOMATOES WITH BASIL & CREAM

3 tablespoons olive oil
1 large onion, peeled and thinly sliced
10 large tomatoes, skinned and thinly sliced
2 teaspoons sugar
1 tablespoon chopped fresh parsley
2 teaspoons chopped fresh basil, or 1 teaspoon
  dried basil, plus a sprig to garnish
salt
freshly ground black pepper
300ml ($\frac{1}{2}$ pint) double cream
75g (3oz) fresh white breadcrumbs
25g (1oz) butter

Preparation time: 30 minutes
Cooking time: 45–50 minutes
Oven: 180°C, 350°F, Gas Mark 4

1. Heat 2 tablespoons oil in a frying pan, and fry the onion slices gently until soft.
2. Brush a baking dish with the remaining oil. Put one-third of the tomato slices in the bottom of the dish and sprinkle with a little sugar, parsley and basil, and salt and pepper to taste. Top with a few onion slices, then pour in about one-third of the cream. Repeat these layers twice more, then sprinkle over the breadcrumbs. Dot with the butter.
3. Bake, uncovered, in a preheated oven for 35–40 minutes, until golden. Serve hot, garnished with a basil sprig.

Serves 4

Nutrition content per serving   Carbohydrate: 22g   Fat: 53g
Fibre: 5g   Kilocalories: 577

COURGETTES CASSEROLED WITH CHEESE

50g (2oz) butter
1 medium onion, peeled and thinly sliced
450g (1lb) courgettes, sliced
2 eggs
300ml ($\frac{1}{2}$ pint) double cream
$\frac{1}{4}$ teaspoon freshly grated nutmeg
salt
freshly ground black pepper
50g (2oz) Gruyère cheese, grated

TOP: Tomatoes with Basil & Cream; BOTTOM: Courgettes Casseroled with Cheese.

Preparation time: about 15 minutes
Cooking time: 40–45 minutes
Oven: 200°C, 400°F, Gas Mark 6

1. Melt half the butter in a large frying pan, add the sliced onion and fry gently until soft. Remove to a buttered ovenproof dish.
2. Melt the remaining butter in the pan, add the courgette slices and fry for about 10 minutes until golden brown on both sides, turning them frequently. Transfer to the dish and mix with the onions.
3. In a bowl, beat the eggs well to mix, then beat in the cream, nutmeg, and salt and pepper to taste. Pour over the courgettes and onions, then sprinkle the cheese evenly over the top.
4. Bake in a preheated oven for 20–25 minutes or until set and golden.

Serves 4

Nutrition content per serving   Carbohydrate: 8g   Fat: 54g
Fibre: 2g   Kilocalories: 556

RED CABBAGE CASSEROLE

2 cooking apples, peeled, cored and sliced
750g (1$\frac{1}{2}$ lb) red cabbage, thinly sliced
1 large onion, peeled and thinly sliced
50g (2oz) raisins
2 teaspoons sugar
salt
freshly ground black pepper
300ml ($\frac{1}{2}$ pint) dry white wine or chicken stock
25g (1oz) butter
lemon slice, to garnish (optional)

Preparation time: 35 minutes
Cooking time: 1 hour
Oven: 180°C, 350°F, Gas Mark 4

1. Put the apples in an ovenproof casserole dish with the red cabbage, onion, raisins, sugar, and salt and pepper to taste. Pour in the wine or stock and stir well to mix.
2. Cover the casserole with a lid or buttered greaseproof paper or foil and bake in a preheated oven for 1 hour or until the cabbage is tender.
3. Remove from oven. Adjust seasoning and stir in the butter until melted. Garnish with a twisted lemon slice, if liked, and serve.

Serves 8

Nutrition content per serving   Carbohydrate: 14g   Fat: 3g
Fibre: 5g   Kilocalories: 85

CASSEROLE OF CHESTNUTS, APPLE & PRUNES

25g (1oz) butter
1 onion, peeled and chopped
225g (8oz) prunes, soaked in water overnight,
*   drained and stoned*
225g (8oz) chestnuts, peeled and cooked
1 large cooking apple, peeled, cored and sliced
1 tablespoon soft brown sugar
300 ml (½ pint) dry red wine
1 cinnamon stick
salt
freshly ground black pepper
TO GARNISH:
crispy fried bacon, crumbled
parsley sprig

Preparation time: 15 minutes, plus soaking
prunes and cooking chestnuts
Cooking time: 1 hour
Oven: 180°C, 350°F, Gas Mark 4

1. Melt the butter in a flameproof casserole,
add the onion and cook until softened.
2. Stir in the prunes, chestnuts, apple, brown
sugar, red wine and cinnamon. Season to taste
with salt and pepper.
3. Bring to the boil, then cover and transfer to
a preheated oven. Cook for 1 hour.
4. Discard the cinnamon stick. Adjust the
seasoning. Garnish with bacon and a parsley
sprig, and serve with duck or game dishes.

Serves 4

Nutrition content per serving   Carbohydrate: 53g   Fat: 12g
Fibre: 14g   Kilocalories: 334

GRATIN OF RICE, TOMATOES & COURGETTES

at least 4 tablespoons olive oil
1 medium onion, peeled and finely chopped
225g (8oz) courgettes, diced
2 eggs
salt
freshly ground black pepper
50–75g (2–3oz) Parmesan cheese, grated
4 tablespoons chopped fresh parsley
4 tablespoons cooked rice
2 tablespoons fresh white breadcrumbs
4 large tomatoes, halved and seeded

Preparation time: 20 minutes
Cooking time: about 25 minutes
Oven: 190°C, 375°F, Gas Mark 5

1. Heat half the olive oil in a pan and fry the
onion gently for 3 minutes.
2. Add the courgettes and cook for a further 5
minutes.
3. Beat the eggs with salt and pepper to taste,
and add the cheese, half the parsley and the
cooked rice. Stir in the onion and courgette
mixture.
4. Spread the vegetable and rice mixture
evenly in a greased ovenproof gratin dish.
5. Mix the remaining chopped parsley with the
breadcrumbs.
6. Push the halved tomatoes, cut sides
uppermost into the rice and vegetable mixture,
easing them down until the tops are level with
the mixture. Sprinkle the parsley and
breadcrumbs over the tomatoes and drizzle the
remaining olive oil evenly over the whole dish
(you may need a little extra olive oil).
7. Bake in a preheated oven for 15–17 minutes.
Serve hot.

Serves 4

Nutrition content per serving   Carbohydrate: 17g   Fat: 26g
Fibre: 3g   Kilocalories: 341

Gratin of Rice, Tomatoes & Courgettes.

BEAN & CABBAGE HOTPOT

Dark red aduki beans are easy to find in
health-food shops. They have a nutty flavour
which blends particularly well with the cabbage
in this meal-in-a-pot recipe.

*175g (6oz) aduki beans, soaked overnight in cold
  water*
1 tablespoon vegetable oil
3 medium onions, peeled and chopped
175g (6oz) carrots, peeled and sliced into rings
350g (12oz) hard white cabbage, shredded
½ teaspoon celery seed
freshly ground black pepper
salt
900ml (1½ pints) hot vegetable stock
TOPPING:
*750g (1½ lb) potatoes, cooked whole in their skins,
  then sliced*
15g (½ oz) butter, melted
paprika, to garnish

Preparation time: 30 minutes, plus soaking
overnight
Cooking time: $1\frac{3}{4}$ hours
Oven: 220°C, 425°F, Gas Mark 7

1. Drain the beans and then rinse under cold
running water. Put them in a pan, cover with
cold water and bring to the boil. Boil fast for
10 minutes then lower the heat. Half cover the
pan and simmer for 35–45 minutes until
tender. Drain, rinse and set aside.
2. Heat the oil in a large pan with a lid and
cook the onions, carrots and cabbage, covered,
for about 5 minutes.
3. Add the celery seed, plenty of black pepper
and a little salt, then pour in the hot stock.
Cover the pan and simmer gently for about 15
minutes then stir in the cooked beans.
4. Spoon the mixture into a large shallow
casserole and arrange the slices of potatoes to
cover the top. Brush with melted butter and
bake in a preheated oven for about 30 minutes
until the potatoes are browned and crisp.
Sprinkle with paprika before serving.

Serves 4

Nutrition content per serving   Carbohydrate: 63g   Fat: 8g
Fibre: 19g   Kilocalories: 365

TOP: Aubergine & Tomato Casserole; BOTTOM: Bean
& Cabbage Hotpot.

AUBERGINE & TOMATO CASSEROLE

This vegetable dish is a delicious creamy blend
of aubergines, tomatoes and yogurt, with a
crisp topping of grated Parmesan cheese.

about 120ml (4fl oz) vegetable oil
*2 large aubergines, about 750g (1½ lb), sliced,
  salted and drained*
1 large onion, peeled and thinly sliced
1 garlic clove, peeled and crushed (optional)
1 × 400g (14oz) can tomatoes, sieved
1 tablespoon tomato purée
*1 teaspoon chopped fresh oregano or basil, or
  ½ teaspoon dried oregano or basil*
½ teaspoon sugar
salt
freshly ground black pepper
150ml (¼ pint) plain unsweetened yogurt
25g (1oz) Parmesan cheese, grated
25g (1oz) fresh white breadcrumbs

Preparation time: 40 minutes
Cooking time: about 1 hour
Oven: 180°C, 350°F, Gas Mark 4

1. Heat 2–3 tablespoons of oil in a large frying
pan. Add enough aubergine slices to cover the
bottom of the pan and fry until browned on
both sides, then remove from the pan with a
slotted spoon and drain on paper towels. Fry
the remaining aubergine slices in this way,
adding more oil when necessary.
2. Fry the onion and garlic (if using) until
golden in the same pan. Stir in the sieved
tomatoes, tomato purée, oregano or basil,
sugar, and salt and pepper to taste. Bring to
the boil, then simmer for 5 minutes.
3. Divide the aubergines into three equal
portions and put one portion in the bottom of a
shallow ovenproof dish. Divide the tomato
sauce into two and put one half on top of the
aubergine layer. Spoon half of the yogurt on
top of the tomato sauce. Repeat these three
layers once more, then finish with the
remaining portion of aubergines.
4. Sprinkle the top with the Parmesan and
breadcrumbs. Bake in a preheated oven for 30
minutes or until golden brown and bubbling.

Serves 4

Nutrition content per serving   Carbohydrate: 16g   Fat: 32g
Fibre: 6g   Kilocalories: 380

CARROT & SWEETCORN CRUMBLE

450g (1lb) carrots, peeled
salt
15g ($\frac{1}{2}$ oz) butter
2 teaspoons clear honey
3 tablespoons chicken stock
freshly ground black pepper
1 × 225g (8oz) can sweetcorn, drained
1 tablespoon chopped fresh parsley
TOPPING:
100g (4oz) plain or wholemeal flour
65g (2$\frac{1}{2}$ oz) butter
25g (1oz) breadcrumbs
a pinch of ground ginger

Preparation time: 30 minutes
Cooking time: 35 minutes
Oven: 190°C, 375°F, Gas Mark 5

1. Cook the carrots in boiling, salted water for 15 minutes, or until they are just tender.
2. Drain and dice them, then mix with the butter, honey, chicken stock and salt and pepper to taste.
3. Spread the carrots in a greased 1 litre (2 pint) baking dish. Cover with the sweetcorn and sprinkle on the parsley.
4. To make the topping, mix the flour with $\frac{1}{2}$ teaspoon salt and rub in the butter until the mixture is like crumbs. Stir in the breadcrumbs and ginger.
5. Sprinkle the topping over the vegetables and cook in a preheated oven for 20 minutes, until the crumble is crisp and brown. Serve hot. A green vegetable such as broccoli in parsley sauce is a good accompaniment.

Serves 4

Nutrition content per serving   Carbohydrate: 40g   Fat: 17g
Fibre: 8g   Kilocalories: 325

BRAISED VEGETABLES WITH CORIANDER

This dish goes particularly well with roast meat or chicken.

25g (1oz) butter
1 large onion, peeled and chopped
3 large heads of celery, trimmed and chopped
1 carrot, peeled and diced
1 parsnip, peeled and diced
300ml ($\frac{1}{2}$ pint) chicken stock or water
2 tablespoons chopped fresh coriander leaves, or
   1 teaspoon ground coriander
pinch of dried thyme
1 tablespoon chopped fresh parsley
salt
freshly ground black pepper
TO SERVE:
2 tablespoons double cream (optional)
1 tablespoon chopped fresh coriander leaves

Preparation time: 10 minutes
Cooking time: 1 hour
Oven: 180°C, 350°F, Gas Mark 4

1. Melt the butter in a flameproof casserole, add the onion and fry until translucent. Add the celery, carrot and parsnip and cook for 5 minutes.
2. Pour over the stock or water and add the herbs and salt and pepper to taste. Cover tightly and cook in a preheated oven for 1 hour.
3. Just before serving, strain off any excess juices and keep for making stock. Pour the cream over the vegetables, if used, and taste and adjust the seasoning. Sprinkle with fresh coriander leaves.

Serves 4

Nutrition content per serving   Carbohydrate: 10g   Fat: 9g
Fibre: 8g   Kilocalories: 133

TOP: Carrot & Sweetcorn Crumble; BOTTOM: Braised Vegetables with Coriander.

Pulse & pasta

CASSEROLES

Pulses – dried beans, peas and lentils – and pasta are very nutritious, and they are cheap. So a casserole based on pulses or pasta is an excellent choice for a family meal. In addition, all of the casseroles in this chapter can be served as main dishes, with perhaps a crisp salad and bread to accompany them, so they are ideal for the busy cook.

You might like to try a substantial dish of lentils and mixed vegetables served topped with sausages, or a layered casserole of buttered noodles, spinach, tomato-pork sauce and cheese sauce. There are two lasagnes to choose from: one with beef and Parma ham meatballs and one with tuna and hard-boiled eggs. You'll also find an egg and macaroni cheese, and ham and vermicelli in a savoury custard.

Hearty Lentil Casserole with Sausages
(see recipe on page 88).

HEARTY LENTIL CASSEROLE WITH SAUSAGES

1 aubergine, chopped
salt
2 tablespoons olive oil
1 onion, peeled and chopped
1 garlic clove, peeled and chopped
4 carrots, peeled and chopped
2 celery sticks, chopped
2 parsnips, peeled and cut into 2.5cm (1inch) strips
225g (8oz) whole green or brown lentils, rinsed
900ml (1½ pints) hot stock or water
1 bay leaf
1 parsley sprig
1 teaspoon dried savory
1 teaspoon dried marjoram
1 teaspoon tomato purée
freshly ground black pepper
225g (8oz) courgettes, thickly sliced
450g (1lb) pork sausages or frankfurters

Preparation time: 20 minutes, plus soaking
Cooking time: about 1¼ hours
Oven: 190°C, 375°F, Gas Mark 5

1. Put the aubergine into a colander. Sprinkle with salt and cover with a plate, weighted down. Leave for at least 30 minutes. Rinse the aubergine and drain on paper towels.
2. Heat the oil in a large flameproof casserole, add the onion and fry until translucent. Add the garlic and aubergine and fry for 5 minutes more. Stir in the carrots, celery, parsnips and lentils and pour over the hot stock or water. Bring to the boil, then boil for 10 minutes.
3. Add the bay leaf, parsley, savory, marjoram, tomato purée and salt and pepper. Cover tightly and cook in a preheated oven for 35 minutes, stirring occasionally.
4. Add the courgettes, with a little more hot stock or water if there isn't enough liquid in the pan. Cover tightly again and cook for a further 15 minutes or until the courgettes are tender and the liquid has been absorbed. Should there be too much liquid, cook uncovered for a few minutes.
5. Meanwhile, cook the sausages.
6. Transfer the vegetable mixture to a warmed serving dish. Arrange the sausages on top.

Serves 4

Nutrition content per serving   Carbohydrate: 57g   Fat: 28g
Fibre: 15g   Kilocalories: 576

TUNA LASAGNE

1 onion, peeled and chopped
25g (1oz) butter
1 tablespoon plain flour
300ml (½ pint) chicken stock
300ml (½ pint) milk
1 × 200g (7oz) can tuna, drained and flaked
salt
freshly ground black pepper
grated rind of ½ lemon
3 hard-boiled eggs
175g (6oz) no-cook lasagne
150ml (¼ pint) double cream
1 egg
2 tablespoons chopped fresh parsley

Preparation time: 30 minutes
Cooking time: 1 hour
Oven: 190°C, 375°F, Gas Mark 5

1. Fry the onion gently in the butter for 3 minutes. Stir in the flour and cook for 1 minute. Remove the pan from the heat and gradually stir in the chicken stock and milk. Bring to the boil, stirring until lightly thickened. Add the tuna, salt and pepper to taste, the lemon rind and one of the hard-boiled eggs, chopped.
2. Layer the sauce and the dry sheets of lasagne in a greased ovenproof dish, starting and finishing with sauce. Bake in a preheated oven for 25 minutes, covered with a piece of greased foil.
3. Beat the cream lightly with the egg and stir in the parsley. Spoon evenly over the lasagne. Thickly slice the remaining hard-boiled eggs and arrange on top. Bake for a further 20 minutes.

Serves 4

Nutrition content per serving   Carbohydrate: 45g   Fat: 44g
Fibre: 1g   Kilocalories: 680

Tuna Lasagne.

LASAGNE WITH MEATBALLS

225g (8oz) lean beef, finely minced
175g (6oz) Parma ham, finely minced
1 small onion, peeled and grated
1 tablespoon chopped fresh sage
1 garlic clove, peeled and crushed
salt
freshly ground black pepper
2 egg yolks
oil for frying
225g (8oz) lasagne
4 tablespoons grated Parmesan cheese
celery leaf, to garnish (optional)
SAUCE:
40g (1½oz) butter
40g (1½oz) plain flour
900ml (1½ pints) milk
175g (6oz) Mozzarella or Bel Paese cheese, diced

Preparation time: 25–30 minutes
Cooking time: about 45 minutes, depending on type of lasagne
Oven: 180°C, 350°F, Gas Mark 4

1. Mix the minced meats with the onion, sage, garlic, salt and pepper to taste, and the egg yolks. Form into small meatballs, about the size of a large olive. Shallow fry the meatballs in oil until lightly browned on all sides. Drain on paper towels.
2. To make the sauce, melt the butter gently in a saucepan, then remove from the heat and stir in the flour. Gradually stir in the milk, then return to the heat and bring to the boil, stirring constantly. Simmer for 3–4 minutes, stirring. Stir in the diced cheese.
3. Lower the lasagne into a large pan of boiling salted water, adding one sheet at a time. Cook at a steady rolling boil – 4 minutes for homemade lasagne, 10–12 minutes for packet lasagne. Drain the cooked lasagne and lay out in single sheets on a wet tea towel (this will prevent the lasagne from sticking).
4. Put a little of the sauce into the base of a greased large shallow rectangular ovenproof dish. Add a layer of lasagne, a few meatballs, and a little more of the sauce. Continue with alternate layers of lasagne, meatballs and sauce, finishing with a layer of sauce. Sprinkle with the grated Parmesan cheese.

TOP: Lasagne with Meatballs; BOTTOM: Special Macaroni Cheese.

5. Place in a preheated oven and bake for 35–40 minutes until golden and bubbling. Serve hot, garnished with a celery leaf, if liked.

Serves 6

Nutrition content per serving   Carbohydrate: 45g   Fat: 36g
Fibre: 0g   Kilocalories: 635

SPECIAL MACARONI CHEESE

225g (8oz) shortcut macaroni
oil
salt
25g (1oz) butter
1 tablespoon plain flour
300ml (½ pint) milk
4 hard-boiled eggs, chopped
freshly ground black pepper
1 large onion, peeled and sliced
75g (3oz) cheese, grated

Preparation time: 20 minutes
Cooking time: 45 minutes
Oven: 200°C, 400°F, Gas Mark 6

1. Put the macaroni in a large pan of boiling water with 1 tablespoon oil and 1 teaspoon salt and cook for 6 minutes.
2. Meanwhile make the white sauce. Melt the butter in a pan, stir in the flour and cook for 30 seconds. Remove the pan from the heat and gradually stir in the milk. Cook over a gentle heat until thickened. Stir in the chopped hard-boiled eggs and add salt and pepper to taste.
3. Drain the cooked macaroni thoroughly and add to the sauce. Spoon into a lightly oiled ovenproof dish or into individual dishes.
4. Fry the sliced onion in a little oil until it starts to brown. Spoon the onion over the macaroni and sprinkle with the grated cheese.
5. Bake in a preheated oven for 15 minutes. Serve immediately with a tomato salad.

Serves 4

Nutrition content per serving   Carbohydrate: 53g   Fat: 26g
Fibre: 1g   Kilocalories: 521

SPAGHETTI LAYER BAKE

2 tablespoons oil
1 large onion, peeled and chopped
450g (1lb) tomatoes, skinned and chopped
100g (4oz) mushrooms, chopped
1 tablespoon tomato purée
1 teaspoon dried oregano
salt
freshly ground black pepper
225g (8oz) minced pork
1 garlic clove, peeled and crushed
175g (6oz) long spaghetti
TOPPING:
25g (1oz) butter
2 tablespoons plain flour
300ml ($\frac{1}{2}$ pint) milk
1 egg, beaten
1 teaspoon dry mustard
75g (3oz) mature Cheddar cheese, grated

Preparation time: 1 hour
Cooking time: 1–1$\frac{1}{4}$ hours
Oven: 190°C, 375°F, Gas Mark 5

1. Heat half the oil in a saucepan. Add the onion and fry until soft. Add the tomatoes, mushrooms, tomato purée, oregano and salt and pepper. Cook for 5 minutes.
2. To make meatballs, mix together the pork, garlic, salt and pepper. With floured hands, shape the mixture into 16 balls.
3. Heat the rest of the oil in a frying pan. Add the pork balls and fry until lightly browned on all sides. Drain on paper towels.
4. Cook the spaghetti in boiling salted water for about 8 minutes or until just 'al dente'. Drain well and add to the tomato sauce.
5. Place half the spaghetti mixture into a 1.75 litre (3 pint) deep casserole. Add the meatballs, then cover with the rest of the spaghetti.
6. To make the topping, melt the butter in a saucepan. Add the flour and cook for 1 minute. Gradually stir in the milk. Bring to the boil, stirring continuously, and cook until thickened and smooth. Remove from the heat and allow to cool slightly. Add the egg, mustard, cheese and seasoning and stir until well blended.
7. Pour the sauce over the top of the spaghetti to cover it completely. Cook in a preheated oven for 1–1$\frac{1}{4}$ hours or until set and browned.

Serves 4

Nutrition content per serving   Carbohydrate: 52g   Fat: 28g
Fibre: 3g   Kilocalories: 571

PASTA & PORK CASSEROLE

25g (1oz) butter, plus 2 knobs
1 large onion, peeled and thinly sliced
350g (12oz) lean minced pork
1 × 400g (14oz) can tomatoes
1 tablespoon medium dry sherry
1 garlic clove, peeled and crushed
$\frac{1}{2}$ teaspoon dried thyme
1 bay leaf
salt
freshly ground black pepper
1 × 450g (1lb) packet frozen whole leaf spinach
175g (6oz) noodles
2 teaspoons cornflour
CHEESE SAUCE:
40g (1$\frac{1}{2}$ oz) butter
40g (1$\frac{1}{2}$ oz) plain flour
450ml ($\frac{3}{4}$ pint) milk
100g (4oz) Cheddar cheese, grated

Preparation time: 30 minutes
Cooking time: about 1$\frac{1}{4}$ hours
Oven: 180°C, 350°F, Gas Mark 4

1. Heat the butter and fry the onion until soft. Add the pork and cook until browned. Stir in the tomatoes, sherry, garlic and herbs. Season and simmer, covered, for 30 minutes.
2. To make the cheese sauce, melt the butter gently, then remove from the heat and stir in the flour. Gradually stir in the milk, then return to the heat and bring to the boil, stirring constantly. Simmer for 3–4 minutes, stirring, then stir in half the cheese and seasoning.
3. Heat the frozen spinach with a knob of butter. When soft, drain well and spread over bottom of a greased ovenproof dish.
4. Cook the noodles in boiling salted water for 5 minutes. Drain and add a knob of butter.
5. Blend the cornflour with a little cold water, stir into the pork and tomato mixture and bring to the boil. Adjust the seasoning.
6. Spoon half the cheese sauce over the spinach, top with the buttered noodles, then meat sauce and the remaining cheese sauce. Sprinkle with the remaining grated cheese and bake in a preheated oven for 30 minutes.

Serves 4

Nutrition content per serving   Carbohydrate: 58g   Fat: 36g
Fibre: 5g   Kilocalories: 702

TOP: Spaghetti Layer Bake; BOTTOM: Pasta & Pork Casserole.

HAM & VERMICELLI POT

225g (8oz) vermicelli, cooked and drained
2 onions, peeled and grated
225g (8oz) cooked ham or bacon, diced
2 tablespoons chopped fresh parsley
salt
freshly ground black pepper
50g (2oz) butter
50g (2oz) plain flour
600ml (1 pint) creamy milk
50g (2oz) Parmesan cheese, grated
2 teaspoons caraway seeds
thin green and red pepper rings, to garnish

Preparation time: 20 minutes
Cooking time: 30 minutes
Oven: 180°C, 350°F, Gas Mark 4

1. Mix together the vermicelli, onion, ham or bacon and parsley. Season with a little salt and plenty of pepper.
2. Melt the butter in a flameproof casserole, stir in the flour and cook gently for 3–4 minutes. Gradually pour in the milk, stirring, and bring to the boil. Simmer for 5 minutes.
3. Stir in the cheese and caraway seeds with salt and pepper to taste. Carefully fold in the vermicelli mixture. Cover the casserole and cook in a preheated oven for 30 minutes.
4. Garnish with the pepper rings and serve with an orange, watercress and almond salad.

Serves 4

Nutrition content per serving   Carbohydrate: 69g   Fat: 26g
Fibre: 2g   Kilocalories: 606

BOSTON BAKED BEANS

450g (1lb) dry white haricot or pinto beans,
  soaked overnight
225g (8oz) salt belly of pork, or a small knuckle
  end of smoked bacon
3–4 tablespoons black treacle, to taste
2 teaspoons dry mustard
pinch of ground ginger
1 teaspoon salt
1 medium onion, peeled
6 cloves

Preparation time: about 20 minutes, plus soaking
Cooking time: about 6 hours
Oven: 120°C, 250°F, Gas Mark ½; then 180°C, 350°F, Gas Mark 4

1. Drain the beans and place in a pan with 1 litre (1¾ pints) of cold water. Bring to the boil, and boil for 2 minutes. Remove from the heat and let them stand, covered, for 2 hours.
2. Blanch the salt pork in boiling water for 5 minutes; drain. Cut into 5cm (2 inch) cubes.
3. Drain the beans, return to the washed-out saucepan, cover with cold water to a depth of 5cm (2 inches), bring to the boil and simmer for about 45 minutes, or until the beans are just tender. Add more water if necessary.
4. Drain the beans and stir in the treacle, to taste, and the mustard, ginger and salt. Stud the onion with cloves and cut into eighths.
5. Put a layer of beans in the bottom of a large casserole, add half the pork cubes, some onion, then the remainder of the beans, pork and onion. Pour in boiling water just to the top, cover tightly and cook in a preheated oven for about 5 hours, adding fresh hot water from time to time if the beans look too dry.
6. Remove the lid, raise the heat and stir the beans to bring some of the salt pork to the top. Bake for a further 45–60 minutes until the pork is brown and crisp.

Serves 6

Nutrition content per serving   Carbohydrate: 42g   Fat: 15g
Fibre: 19g   Kilocalories: 383

LEFT: Ham & Vermicelli Pot.
RIGHT: Boston Baked Beans.

INDEX